The World's Best Ever Strikers

Mirsad Hasic

DEDICATION

I dedicate this book to my wife.

CONTENTS

ACKNOWLEDGMENTS

I would like to thank my family for their support.

Introduction

All my life I've been a soccer fan. For as long as I can recall, I was that kid spending all his time playing soccer, watching soccer, or spend the night thinking about soccer with posters of famous players handing on the walls around my bed.

For me, soccer was a serious thing and I sometimes found it difficult to understand how some people don't like it the way I did - and still do - or carry the same passion I've always carried towards it.

I simply didn't find a reason why someone not to be a serious fan for Ronaldo – the real Ronaldo – or not debating about who's England's best, Arsenal or Manchester or even not being aware of a new talent in my country called Zlatan Ibrahimović.

Those people were somehow aliens to me since, to me, soccer was a magical world with real men shedding blood sweat and tears to draw smiles on the faces of similar, obsessed, people chanting around while watching the 22 run after a tiny little thing on a 60X100m ground.

Yes, I'm fanatic and proud, and I'd like to share my passion for the game with you in this book. My name is Mirsad Hasic, a soccer coach and ex player, and in this book, I'd like to take you on a long, exciting tour inside the lives of the greatest attackers who ever played the beautiful game. So without further ado, let's get started.

Ronaldo - Il Fenomeno (Phenomen)

Full Name: Ronaldo Luís Nazário de Lima
Date of birth: 18 September 1976
Nationality: Brazilian
Status: Retired in 2011
Clubs: Cruzeiro, Corinthians (Brazil) – Barcelona, Real Madrid (Spain) - Inter Milan, AC Milan (Italy) - PSV Eindhoven (Netherland)
Goals scored and number of games: 414 goals in 616 games
Goals scored internationally: 62 goals in 98 Caps
Club Trophies:
- Europa League: 1998 (Inter Milan)
- UEFA Cup Winners' Cup: 1997 (Barcelona)
- Spanish league (La Liga): 2002-2003 (Real Madrid)
- Spanish Cup: 1997 (Barcelona)
- Spanish Super Cup: 1996 (Barcelona) and 2003 (Real Madrid)
- Brazilian Cup: 1993 (Cruzeiro) and 2009 (Corinthians)
- Dutch Cup: 1996 (PSV)

National Team Trophies:
- FIFA World Cup: 1994 & 2002
- FIFA Confederations Cup: 1997
- Copa America: (1997, 1999)

Personal Trophies:
- FIFA World Player of the Year: 3 times (1996, 1997, 2002)
- FIFA Ballon d'Or: Twice (1997, 2002)
- FIFA World Cup Golden Boot: 1998 – 2002
- Brazil national soccer team Hall of Fame: 2006
- Real Madrid Hall of fame: 2011

- Italian Soccer Hall of Fame: 2015
- Spanish league top scorer (El Pichichi): twice (1996–1997, 2003-2004)
- Dutch league top scorer: (1994 -1995)
- Italy's Soccerer of the year: 1997–98
- Serie A (the Italian league) Player of the Decade: 1997–2007
- Copa America's best player: (1997)

Career Overview

Ronaldo started his career at eleven; playing for Sao Cristovao for three years after his mother

broke up with his alcoholic father who was the one who encouraged little Ronaldo, or Ronaldinho, to keep playing soccer despite his mother's objections.

Ronaldo began to grab attention right after he joined his second club "Curzeiro" with which he scored 44 goals during his first 47 games, forcing Brazil's manager – Carlos Alberto Parreira - to offer him a place in team heading to USA for the 1994 World Cup.

In USA, and despite not playing at any game, Ronaldo convinced everyone on the team he is sooner to be the best player in Brazil within just a few years, and following Romario's advice, he joined PSV Eindhoven for 6 million dollars to train under the eyes of England's legendary coach; Sir Bobby Robson.

With PSV, Ronaldo managed to score a whole of 54 goals during his 57 games with the Dutch giants, but a world record fee of 13.2 million

Euros secured a move to Spain, to join Barcelona alongside with Robson who watched his wonder kid, again, score a whole litany of goals that reached 47 in his first and only 49 games for Barça including Ronaldo's famous goal against FC Compostela, dribbling past 6 players and their goalkeeper before scoring one of the most beautiful goals in the history of La Liga.

That year, 1997, Ronaldo helped Barça win the Spanish Cup and was set to sign an extended contract with the team, but a few problems prior to signing this contract made him decide to move to Inter which paid his release clause fee and signed him for another transfer record of 19.5 million Euros.

In 98, he proved himself as a successful signing for Inter, scoring 34 goals in 47 games, including a third goal in their 3-0 win against Lazio at the UEFA Cup final.

That night, Ronaldo proved himself against, one of the Italy's best defenders of all times, Alessandro Nesta, forcing him to use everything, including beating, for the hope of stopping the Brazilian who refused to end the game without scoring a remarkable goal twenty minutes before the final whistle.

A month later, he won the best player in the World Cup after participating in 7 goals for the Brazilian team however, a late injury 24 hours before the championship's final prevented Ronaldo from doing his magic and score against the French team that won the final by 3 goals.

The 3 seasons between 1998 and 2002 were the hardest on Ronaldo with two serious knee injuries forced him to spend more than 20 months without in the hospital unable to play.

However he managed to make a remarkable comeback one month before the World Cup, and lead Brazil with its famous 4R team – Ronaldo, Rivaldo, Ronaldinho and, Roberto Carlos – to win the tournament after scoring 8 goals, including his famous double against Germany in the final.

Those 8 goals helped him win both the FIFA player of the year and the Ballon d'Or, in addition to the World Cup golden boot. That lured Real Madrid's president, Florentino Pérez, to sign him and make him part of his Galacticos team.

In summer 2002, Ronaldo officially joined the other Spanish giant helping the team win one league title and one Super cup in 3 years, scoring some of the most amazing goals, including a famous hat-trick against Man United in the 2003 Champions League.

However, after favoring Ruud van Nistelrooy over him in 2006, Ronaldo paid asked for a move back to Italy to join AC Milan which happened summer 2006,right after becoming the all-time top scorer of the World Cup the day he scored his 15th championship goal against Ghana in the Round of 16 game.

Milan, Corinthians, and Retirement

After joining Kaka in Milan, Ronaldo started his campaign in Milan with 7 goals in his first 14 games.

Unfortunately he spent the rest of his contract with Milan suffering from a set of serious injuries got him to think about returning back to Brazil after not getting a new contract from Milan.

In 2009, he returned back to homeland, to spend one successful year with Corinthians, helping the team win both the Campeonato Paulista and the Super cup, with 23 goals in 38 game.

He then followed his successful year with 12 more goals in 2010 however, after ending the season trophy-less and suffering from weight problems and another knee injury, Ronaldo chose to retire in 2011, only 2 years after the man who said the following words died.

"Ronaldo? Had he managed to stay free of injury, he would become the best soccer player ever." Sir Bobby Robson

Performance

Ronaldo was one of the kind and a lot of people wouldn't disagree if you claimed that he was the best striker ever.

1-on-1 Genius

When they once asked Zidane how it was to play with Ronaldo he said these words:

"Ronaldo was really amazing when facing his opponents in 1-on-1 duels. Also, what impressed me most is his ability to figure out what his next move is going to be even before the ball reaches his feet"

I don't remember Ronaldo wasting a chance anytime he was alone with the goalkeeper. His two key factors for achieving this were balance and speed.

No matter how tiny the space between him and the goalie, his ability to move the ball between his feet while adjusting his body to always keep the ball close to the foot he decides to shoot with.

No keeper could guess where Ronaldo was going, or what he was about to do next with the ball. He had all his tricks ready to pick from, one day he would feint and do a Pedala against Ghana in the World Cup, then the next day he would do a Flip Flap move, or simply rotate the ball behind his body like his non-famous goal against Getafe.

It's known by every attacker, the easiest way to escape the goalkeeper is to move away from him using the one foot that carries the ball. This means an attacker should make a sudden move to the right when the ball is at his right foot and go left with the left foot.

That day against Getafe, Ronaldo decided to do the opposite. With the ball at his right foot and three defenders close to him, he used his right foot to move the ball behind his body and meeting it with his left to score a goal for Barcelona. It looked easy, but it's one of the hardest moves to do on a breakaway.

He Could Shoot From Anywhere

As he grew older – and, as a way to avoid more injuries - Ronaldo relied more and more on shooting from long distances to create danger on opponents.

Since he joined Inter, he proved himself to be one of the best players in the world to score from almost anywhere in and outside the penalty area.

That night when he scored a hat-trick in the Old Trafford, two of the 3 goals were scored from long distances, the first was from a very tight angle on the far right side of United's penalty area, and the second was a strong long shot from 27 yards above the hands of Fabian Barthez.

He had the ability to simply swing his body, and send the ball wherever he wanted in a blink of an eye, the exact same way he did when scoring for Madrid against Rayo Vallecano.

That day, he wasn't in a good position to score, with two defenders behind, but he twisted his body and send a strong curvy ball out of nowhere. This is what exactly meant by Ibrahimović when describing his childhood hero, he said:

"Ronaldo was incredibly fast and he could actually score from barely nothing while keeping the ball at his feet more skillful than anyone I've ever encountered before"

Alan Shearer - The Well'ard

Full Name: Alan Shearer

Date of birth: 13 August 1970

Nationality: English

Status: Retired (2006)

Clubs: Southampton, Blackburn Rovers and Newcastle United (England)

Goals scored and number of games: 409 goals in 797 games

Goals scored internationally:30 goals in 63 Caps

Club Trophies:

- Premier League winner: 1994–95 (Blackburn Rovers)

National Team Trophies:

- None

Personal Trophies:

- English Premier League top goal scorer of all times :260 goals in 441 games since 1992-1993
- Euro 1996 Golden Boot
- Premier League top goal scorer: 3 times 1994–95, 1995–96, 1996–97
- FIFA's list of 100 greatest soccerers of all times
- Ballon d'Or: Third place 1996
- Newcastle United's greatest player of all times
- Best player in England: 1994–95
- Most Premier League goals scored in season

Career Overview

Born in 1970 in Newcastle, and after being declined by his favorite club, Alan Shearer started his career in the youth academy of Southampton, one of the best English soccer academies in, and the one that introduced to the world players like Gareth Bale, Theo Walcott, Adam Lalana and Alex Oxlade-Chamberlain.

Shearer's physical strength gave him the chance to make his first team debut with the Saints in spring 1988 against Chelsea, a short time before scoring a hat-trick against Arsenal in St Mary's Stadium which was his key to consistently play with Southampton.

He was sold to Blackburn Rovers in summer 1992 despite being so close to joining Alex Ferguson's side at Manchester United however, the presence of Liverpool's legend, Kenny Dalglish, on the head of Blackburn's managerial team made the deal change from the city of Manchester to Lancashire, home of the Rovers.

Winning The League With Blackburn Rovers

The highlight of Shearer's career was in season 1994-95 when he helped the Rovers to win their first league title since the 1913-14 season, and become the only team outside the English "Big Four" to win the league under its new name "The Premier League."

That year, Shearer formed a formidable duo with the newcomer, Chris Sutton, scoring a total of 49 league goals (34 goals were scored by Shearer) to finish the league one point ahead of former champion, Manchester United, despite losing 2–1 to Liverpool on the last day

In total, Shearer spent 4 successful years in Blackburn, scoring 130 goals in all competitions with a conversion rate of goal every 118 minutes, better than any other player in the league.

He then joined his childhood hero, Kevin Keegan, who's now the manager of Newcastle United to help the club win the league they lost to Man United in 1995-96 after finishing second only 4 points behind Alex Ferguson, who again wanted to sign Shearer that summer, but playing with Keegan was more seductive to Shearer.

Newcastle till The End

With Newcastle, and despite failing to win any considerable title, Shearer spent 10 of his best years playing for his boyhood team, proving his loyalty against all temptations to leave Newcastle and join other big teams.

Performance

Shearer mastered the goal scoring both with his head and feet which is exceptional and made him unique in the game of soccer.

A World Class Finisher

The key factor for becoming the all-time goal scorer of one of the most competitive leagues in the world while playing for mid-table teams like Newcastle United and Blackburn Rovers was Shearer's superb finishing skills.

Though managers of these teams gave orders to his teammates to serve him frequently, the only way for Shearer to score 260 league goals was missing less, and making benefit or whatever chances he got to score, since the quality of players around him, no offense, lacked the creativity and the ability to supply him with a continued flow of chances.

With all respect to the players Shearer played next to them, they weren't like Ryan Giggs, Steve McManaman, or Dennis Bergkamp, the best playmakers in England at that time.

King of Diving Headers

Up until now, Alan Shearer is still the best English attacker in air plays. At any condition and from all positions, diving or vertically-jumping, Shearer was so great at headers that it became his trademark.

He has two very famous diving headers in his career, one against Bayern Leverkusen in the Champions league, but technically, the best of them all was in 1994, against USA in a friendly game.

The cross was played poorly, the ball was at knee-height, and the only way to create danger was trying to shoot the ball and bend it outside-in towards the American goal.

But rather than this, Shearer went all towards the ball, got his head down and swerved the ball with his head and sent it in the net.

His ability to use his head instead of his foot was more than amazing, which gave him an edge over other defenders, because when the ball isn't high enough or low enough it raises questions, whether to meet the ball with head or foot, and this split of a second is what any well-trained header like Shearer needs.

Like the day when he scored a magnificent diving header against Coventry City in the English league.

The cross was sent towards the penalty area, the ball came towards his chest, and while 2 defenders were watching, Shearer bent his head, twisted his body and put a strong ball on the right side of the keeper as if it was sent by one of his feet.

The Love for the Magpies

It's rare to see a great player like Shearer spends the great majority of his career in one, non-competitive club.

Until now, people keep asking, why Shearer refused to join Manchester United and Sir Alex Ferguson not once, but twice, and joined Blackburn and Newcastle instead.

It's love that got him to spend the best of his years playing for Newcastle United. This love was probably one of the keys to why Shearer did so well with The Magpies.

Shearer was born and raised in Newcastle watching great players like Kevin Keegan wear the shirt of his favorite team. As a young kid, all he wished for was playing for Newcastle and make himself and his family proud.

Even when he failed to join the club as a kid and went to Southampton's youth academy, that wish didn't fade, until he was asked by Keegan – now the coach of Newcastle – to join the team, a move to Newcastle for him was better than playing for Man United, the most successful English team of that era.

To be willing to give everything for his favorite team was, in my opinion, one of the reasons why Alan Shearer is one of the best soccer players in the past 30 years.

Filippo Inzaghi - Super Pippo

Full Name: Filippo Inzaghi

Date of birth: 9 August 1973

Nationality: Italian

Status: Retired since 2012

Clubs:Piacenza - AlbinoLeffe - Verona - Parma - Atalanta - Juventus - AC Milan (Italy)

Goals scored and number of games: 313 goals in 680 games

Goals scored internationally: 25 goals in 57 Caps

Club Trophies:

- UEFA Champions League: Twice 2002–03, 2006–07 (Milan)
- UEFA Super Cup: Twice 2003, 2007
- FIFA Club World Cup: 2007
- Italian league (Serie A): Twice 2003–04, 2010–11 (Milan)
- Italian Cup: 2002–03 (Milan)
- Italian Super Cup: Twice 2004, 2011 (Milan)

National Team Trophies:

- FIFA World Cup: 2006
- UEFA Euro Cup: 2000 Silver Medalist

Personal Trophies:

- Serie A top scorer: 1996–97 (Atalanta)
- Italy and AC Milan's all time goal scorer in all European champions

Career Overview

Inzaghi started his career in the second division with Piacenza in 1991.

He spent 4 years with the team, scoring 44 goals in 102 games and helping them win the Serie-B before he chose to move and play for Parma, one of the strongest teams in Italy during that time, in summer 1995.

However, despite playing alongside some of Italy's young talents like Gianluigi Buffon and Hernan Crespo, the move to Parma wasn't successful, as Inzaghi netted only twice in 15 league games, something that convinced the club to accept the offer they received from the 13th of the league, Atalanta in summer 1996.

But, this move was later regretted by Parma's executives who watched their man score 24 goals the next season, get picked as the best young talent in Italy, and keep his new team from relegation after finishing 10th in the league (they relegated the next season when Inzaghi left them).

With that performance, Inzaghi became target for Juventus and eventually signed for the team in summer 1997, and later that year, he won both the Serie-A and the Italian Super cup, scoring 27 goals in all competitions, including 2 goals in the super cup game.

The next year though, with the absence of Del Piero, Juventus ended the season trophy-less despite the 20 goals scored by Inzaghi who, despite his later 42 goals, found himself benched for the newcomer David Trezeguet, which made him choose to move to Milan, and join his former coach in Juventus, Carlo Ancelotti.

Making history With AC Milan

Upping to Ancelotti's expectations, Inzaghi finished his first season with Milan scoring 16 goals in 28 games, however his second one was amazing, with 30 goals scored, including 12 goals in the Champions League which he won after defeating his former club on penalties in Manchester United's Old Trafford.

He then helped Milan win the European Super against Porto after finishing on top of the league in 2004 for the first time since 1999.

The highlight of Inzaghi's career though was in 2007 when he scored 5 goals in 3 consecutive cup finals, the Champions league, the European Super and FIFA Club World Cup, the first two of them were in Milan's revenge against Liverpool post the latter's famous comeback in Turkey in the 2005 Champions league final game.

Since 2009, Super Pippo's performance declined out of age (now 36 years old) and injury, and he retired alongside his best friend, Gennaro Gattuso, one year after winning their last league title with Milan in 2011.

Performance

Inzaghi was not the fastest, strongest or posed the most powerful shots, but he was probably one of the most clever strikers to ever enter the soccer field.

The Game's Smartest Student

Inzaghi surely wasn't the best among his peers, not even the best in Milan, but with no doubt, he was among the smartest, if not THE smartest.

He wasn't the strongest, and he wasn't the most skilled, yet all his moves and all the goals he scored proved how much of a smart player he was, and how he made use of everything he had.

The 4th most scoring player in the history of all European championships – and the first prior to the coming of Messi and Ronaldo – might not be seen the same way people perceive the Brazilian Ronaldo.

He may also not be as skilled as him, yet he knew what he was good at, and kept doing it, over and over, and over again. These are what differentiated Inzaghi from the rest of the world:

King of Follow-ups and lost Balls

I have watched Inzaghi's all 126 goals with Milan, only one of the was scored from outside the penalty area, actually it was so close to the area that you could barely count it as a long shot.

If this can prove anything then it's Inzaghi's big brains, and special foresight. He had the skill of successfully guessing where the next ball will be played, or where the defender/keeper will deflect the next shot, and he would position himself to receive that ball.

It's to score when the goal is empty of his keeper, but it's not easy to be in the right place, at the right time, not just once or twice, but 313 times.

Inzaghi was a great student of the game. Like quoted by his teammates, he used to spend nights studying his next opponent, the defenders and the goalkeeper and know everything about them. Like what Gennaro Gattuso said about him:

"A lot of people believed in that Pippo were just at the right place at the right time; however, this has nothing to do with this. Instead, he spent a lot of time to prepare for the upcoming opponents figuring out their weak spots and planning how to take advantage of them."

The Offside Trick

"That lad must have been born offside."

Sir Alex Ferguson, on Filippo Inzaghi's famous ability to beat the offside trap and score

Inzaghi's best trick was playing against the odds. He would break the offside six, seven or even 10 times in one game until the defenders of the other team believe they're playing against an amateur who doesn't know how to position himself properly.

He simply keeps putting himself in the offside until they lose guard, and waiting for one moment when he's in the onside where he could score.

He had this done in the Champions League final against Liverpool, when he received a through behind 4 Liverpool defenders, gave his back to Jamie Carragher - who waved to the lineman for the offside- and scored his second goal in the game.

Thierry Henry - Titou

Full Name: Thierry Daniel Henry
Date of birth: 17 August 1977
Nationality: French
Status: Retired (2014)
Clubs: Arsenal (England) - Juventus (Italy) - Monaco (France) - Barcelona (Spain) - New York Red Bull (USA)
Goals scored and number of games: 411 goals in 915 games
Goals scored internationally: 51 goals in 123 Caps (France's all time goal scorer)

Club Trophies

- UEFA Champions League: 2008 – 2009 (Barcelona)
- UEFA Super Cup: 2009 (Bacelona)
- FIFA Club World Cup: 2009 (Barcelona)
- English Premier League: Twice 2001–02, 2003–04 (Arsenal)
- Spanish League (La Liga): Twice 2008–09, 2009–10 (Barcelona)
- French League (League 1): 1996–97 (Monaco)
- FA Cup: Three times 2001–02, 2002–03, 2004–05
- Spanish Cup (Copa del Rey): 2008–09
- Spanish Super Cup: 2009
- English Super Cup (Community Shield): Twice 2002, 2004
- French Super Cup: 1997

International Trophies:

- FIFA World Cup: 1998
- UEFA European Championship: 2000
- FIFA Confederations Cup: 2003

- FIFA World Cup: Silver Medalist 2006

Personal Trophies:

- Premier League Golden Boot: 4 times: 2001–02, 2003–04, 2004–05, 2005–06
- European Golden Boot: Twice 2003–04, 2004–05
- FIFA Greatest 100 soccerers of all time : 2004
- French Player of the Year: 5 times
- Onze d'Or: Twice 2003, 2006
- Ballon d'Or : Second place: 2003
- Ballon d'Or : Third place: 2006
- FIFA World Player of the Year : Second place twice 2003, 2004
- English Soccer Hall of Fame : 2008
- Arsenal's greatest player of all times: 2012

Career Overview

Maybe you haven't seen him with Arsenal, but what Henry did with Barcelona was unforgettable – even though it was nothing compared to what he was doing in Arsenal.

Thierry Henry was the player you like to watch. The style, the speed, the brains and the leadership skills he had made him one of the best attackers in the history of soccer.

Henry – who played for five different clubs throughout his career – started at an early age at AS Monaco in France before moving to Juventus only a few months after he won the World Cup with France being the youngest player in the history of Les Bleus to win a major trophy.

Unfortunately, that move was unsuccessful as young Henry had very hard time adapting to life in Italy and the tactical, defensive style of soccer there.

He was forced to play on the wing, sometimes Carlo Ancelotti made him play as a defensive midfielder with limited space for creativity which prevented him from scoring more than 3 goals in the 19 appearances he had with The Old Lady.

When he met with his mentor, Arsene Wenger, on a plane in summer 1999, he was convinced by the French coach to leave Juventus and join Arsenal to succeed their all-time goal scorer, Ian Wright, who left the club a year before.

And in August 3rd, 1999, Arsenal signed Thierry Henry for a 5-year deal. And the rest was history.

In Arsenal, it took Henry 8 games after changing his on-field position from the wing to play as a center forward, and it took him another 8, but this time in years, to break Ian Wright's record.

Henry become historic goal scorer of the club with 226 goals, including 175 league goals to become the best foreign attacker in the history of the English Premier league and the 3rd most scoring player behind Alan Shearer and Wayne Rooney.

In addition to his goal scoring skills, Henry holds a standing record for the most number of assists made by one player in one year (23), which he achieved in 2002-2003 despite playing as a center forward.

He also helped Arsenal become the only club in more than 100 years to ever spend an entire season unbeaten. This happened in the 2003-04 season after scoring 30 goals in 37 games, to end the year raising the one and only golden title ever won by an English team.

Leaving Arsenal

After both losing the UEFA champions league against Barcelona, and losing to Italy the World Cup final in the matter of two months.

Because of this Henry decided to leave Arsenal to win the Champions league title, something he knew he won't be able to do with his favorite club heading through a major 5-year budget reduction in order to leave their old stadium "Highbury" and move to a bigger one.

All that made Henry – with lots of tears – move to Barcelona where he managed to win his first, and last, Champions league title, and help the team score 6 goals against their ultimate rival – Real Madrid – in a game that witnessed Henry score twice in Santiago Bernabéu.

In 2010 and after 3 years in Barcelona; Henry moved to USA to play for New York Red Bulls for 4 consecutive years that witnessed some of his greatest goals including a wonderful direct-corner goal against Columbus Crew SC.

With France

With his national team; Henry proved himself as one of the best players in the history of the French team being one of the few to play in 2 World I Cup finals in addition to winning EURO in 2000 after defeating Italy 2-1 in Amsterdam.

Henry is also France's all time goal scorer with 51 goals in 123 games. And is one of the few – alongside legends like, Maradona, Di Stefano, Pavel Nedved and Gianluigi Buffon – who didn't win the Ballon d'Or award despite their great performances.

Henry officially retired in 2014 and he's currently the attacking coach for Arsenal's U-18 team under the supervision of his mentor Arsene Wenger, hoping that he could one day manage the team that witnessed his glory days as one of the best attacking players in the history of soccer.

Performance

Henry was a great player and a goal scoring machine, yet he rarely scored from a header.

Some say this was a disadvantage, but why exhaust yourself in the box dealing with strong, aggressive defenders when you're not born for it?

Thierry Henry wasn't the Ibrahimović-Hulk type of players, but the things he had up in his sleeves, speed and intelligence, were enough for him to build a successful soccer career.

Intelligence

Ever watched any of Henry's goals with NY Red Bulls?

No.

Then let me tell you what happened.

At both, Monaco and Arsenal, pace was Henry's gig, and he used it pretty well to score goals (I will talk about this in the next point), as he grew older, he had to find new ways to score goals. He can't just receive the ball near the center a flash himself between defenders like he did at Arsenal.

He can't do this anymore, even if he tried, he would burn himself out, and you can't do that in the MLS after they pay you zillions of dollars to bring you from Europe and make you the star of the team.

So, what did he do?

He didn't learn something new, at the end of the day he's King Henry who already has it all. He just started relying on his brains more often. You would start seeing goals from corner kicks, sticking to the penalty area more than ever, and playing on defenders' mistakes.

And he did the same thing when he went back to Arsenal, during his historical loan-journey in 2012:

In his comeback game against Leeds United, he came in 25 minutes before the end of the game when it was 0-0, and only needed 10 minutes to do what the rest of his "younger" attacking mates failed to do.

He simply and amazingly, positioned himself between Leeds's defenders, artistically controlled a through ball and bam.... 1-0 for Arsenal.

Another moment of intelligence was against Manchester United in 2000.

The two teams were the only ones competing for the league title at that time, and a game like that was important to win especially for Arsenal since it was a home game.

The game was tough, Man United wanted to keep things at bay, and a draw was good for them so they stuck to their own half and killed all roads to their goal, until one moment when Henry summed up all his greatness in one shot.

He knew United's goalkeeper, Fabian Barthez, they played together in the national team and Henry knew that Barthez was short (only 1.83 m) and not good at long shots.

So what did he do?

He got one ball by the edge of the penalty area, gave Barthez his back, and played an out-of-nowhere long ball above his head to score one of the best and most memorable goals in the history of the English Premier League.

Speed

"When discussing cars you talk about them going from zero to sixty in just a few seconds, and Henry is just like a car."- Peter Beardsley, former Newcastle United player.

Probably this was one of the reasons why Renault chose Henry to be the company's new face in England and do their famous "Va Va Voom" campaign. Just like a car, Henry had pace.

Except for Arjen Robben – and maybe Mohammed Slah – Henry can outrun any of today's fast players, including both Messi and Ronaldo.

Sounds exaggerating?

No I'm not.

In the late 90s, Roberto Carlos was the speed icon in soccer. Anyone ever had a Play Station 1 would put the Brazilian left back at the front because of his shooting power and amazing speed. He was literally, the fastest man in soccer. Yet, each time Henry played against him, he would outrun him.

In fact, in one game between France and Brazil, Henry got Carlos run the entire field after him and he barely touched him.

This kind of pace was crucial for Henry's success – at least in Arsenal. He would start an attack from anywhere on the field, and you'd be lucky if you ever get close to him. They once asked Chelsea's playing manager how to stop Henry, and his answer was quite simple and expressive.

He said:

With a Gun…

Eusébio - The Black Pearl

Full Name: Eusébio da Silva Ferreira

Date of birth: 25 January 1942

Nationality: Portuguese

Status: Died at the age of 71 (5th January 2014)

Clubs: Sporting de Lourenço Marques (Mozambique) - Benfica, Beira-Mar and União de Tomar (Portugal) - Boston Minutemen, New Jersey Americans and Las Vegas Quicksilvers (USA) - Monterrey (Mexico) - Toronto Metros-Croatia (Canada)

Goals scored and number of games: 621 goals in 639 games

Goals scored internationally: 41 goals in 64 Caps

Club Trophies:

- UEFA Champions League (Benfica)
- Portuguese Premier League: 11 times (Benfica)
- Portuguese Cup: 5 times (Benfica)
- Mozambican Soccer Championship: 1960
- NASL (Equivalent to current MLS): 1976

International Trophies:

- FIFA World Cup: Bronze medalist (1966)

Personal Trophies:

- FIFA World Cup Golden Boot: 1966
- Ballon d'Or: 1966
- European Golden Boot: Twice 1968, 1973
- Portuguese Soccerer of the Year: 1970, 1973
- World Soccer's list of the 100 Greatest Soccerers of All Time

Career Overview

Eusebio da Silva Ferreira was born in 1942, to an Angolan -Mozambican couple. Born in such poor conditions, especially after the death of his father in 1950, young Eusebio started playing soccer barefoot in Maputo until he was accepted by Sporting Clube de Lourenço Marques, a nursery club that followed the other Portuguese giants, Sporting Lisbon.

Since he joined the club at the age of 15, Eusebio was the superstar of Clube de Lourenço Marques, scoring a remarkable count of 41 goals in only 22 games with the team, followed by another 36 goals in 20 league games that won the title for the club.

That performance grabbed the attention of scouts from Juventus, Sao Paolo, and Benfica who eventually convinced his family to agree on a 5-year deal.

Yet, there was a huge problem which was convincing the other rival, Sporting Lisbon, to let go of their young player who officially belonged to them on behalf of their Mozambican breeding team.

For that, Eusebio spent his first 5 months in Portugal in a hidden place and with a fake name, Antonio Ferreira, until Sporting people finally agreed to let Benfica have who would later become the best player the history of both Benfica and Portugal.

During the 15 years he played for "The Reds" Eusebio scored 473 goals in 440 games, helped the team win 11 league titles, as well as reach the European Cup final 5 times between 1961 and 1968 including a 3-2 win against Barcelona in 1961 and a 5-3 win against Real Madrid in a game that witnessed Eusebio scoring 2 goals in 3 minutes.

Internationally; Eusebio scored 41 goals in the 64 international appearances making him Portugal's leading goal scorer for 50 consecutive years until his record was broken by Cristiano Ronaldo in 2013, yet he remains the only Portuguese player to win the golden boot in the World Cup after scoring 9 goals in England's 1966 tournament.

Performance

Highly poisoning inside the penalty box while able to drible past any defender, was one of the characteristics of Eusebio

The Powerful Black Panther

Eusebio was one of the strongest players of his generation, if not the strongest. He had the perfect mix of speed that enabled him to outrun almost any defender around him (he could run the 100m in 11 seconds) and the physical strength to handle tackling and beating without losing the ball.

This made extracting the ball from him a hard job for any defender playing against him.Of course, it made him very dangerous in and out the penalty area.

But power alone is never enough

One could see the determination in his eyes anytime he had a shot on target. The struggles he faced and the suffering he has been to while being raised in extreme poverty in Mozambique and watching his father die when he was 8. This all affected Eusebio as a player in a very positive way, and gave him determination..

I have never witnessed someone ever kicking the ball with such determination, not even Messi, Cristiano or the Brazilian Ronaldo, no matter near or far, a penalty or a regular shot, Eusebio put power behind almost all of his shots, he only missed 5 penalties in his career.

Each and every time he kicked the ball it seemed like he was forcing the ball to enter, as if he was saying to it:

You must get in...

And it always did.

Compared to the number of games he played, Eusebio has a conversion rate of 1.02 goals per game. In 715 games he played in more than 20 years, he scored 727 goals including 473 goals with Benfica. And for many, he's the best Portuguese player in history, even better than Ronaldo who scored 532 goals in 784 games.

Different times maybe, but for many, playing for Benfica isn't like playing with Man United or Real Madrid with the best players in the world around to help

Eusebio's determination showed itself in many historical comebacks, including the one when Benfica played in the Club World Cup against Santos and its superstar, Pele.

Santos was 4-0 ahead when young Eusebio entered the field…It took him only 18 minutes to score a hat-trick and win a penalty for his team that was later missed.

Another historical moment was his one-man-comeback against North Korea in the elimination round of the 1966 World Cup. Eusebio scored 4 times and flipped the table on the North Koreans who were leading the score board with 3 goals to zero for Portugal.

Marco van Basten - San Marco

Full Name: Marcel van Basten
Date of birth: 31 October 1964
Nationality: Dutch
Status: Retired too early (1995)
Clubs: Ajax (Netherland) – AC Milan (Italy)
Goals scored and number of games: 300 goals in 431 games
Goals scored internationally: 24 goals in 58 Caps
Club Trophies:
- UEFA Champions League: 2 "Consecutive" times 1988–89, 1989–90 (AC Milan)
- UEFA Cup Winners' Cup: 1986 – 1987 (Ajax)
- UEFA Super Cup: Twice 1989, 1990 (AC Milan)
- Italian League (Serie A): 4 Times 1987–88, 1991–92, 1992–93, 1993–94
- Dutch League (Eredivisie): 3 Times 1981–82, 1982–83, 1984–85
- Dutch Cup: 3 Times 1982–83, 1985–86, 1986–87
- Italian Super Cup: 4 Times 1988, 1992, 1993, 1994

National Team Trophies:
- Euro 88: Winner

Personal Trophies:
- Ballon d'Or: 3 Times 1988, 1989, 1992
- Onze d'Or: Twice 1988, 1989
- World Soccer Player of the Year: Twice 1988, 1992
- Italy's top scorer: Twice 1989–90, 1991–92
- Dutch Soccerer of the Year: 1984–85

- Dutch League top scorer: 4 Times 1983–84, 1984–85, 1985–86, 1986–87

Career Overview

Van Basten started his youth career at the age of seven in EDO, before moving a year later to UVV Utrecht, the same team he spent 9 years with the team before moving to Elinkwijk, then Ajax whose reps saw a new Johan Cruyff in young Marco who didn't play much at first.

He only made 2 appearances during his first season in Amsterdam. However, the young forward started showing himself the next year scoring 13 goals in 25 games and helping the Dutch giants win their second Eredivisie title in a row.

The next year though was the year Van Basten cracked the code to the hearts of Ajax fans, scoring 29 goals in 38 games despite losing their league title to Feyenoord which won the double that year, 1984.

The highlight of Van Basten's career with Ajax was in the 1986-87 season, when he managed to score 43 goals in 43 games helping Ajax win the Dutch cup as well as their first and only European Cup Winners Cup after scoring an early winner against Lokomotive Leipzig in the final game played in Athens.

Joining The Mighty AC Milan

After an era of problems, including relegating twice to the second division (1980, 1982), Silvio Berlusconi became president to AC Milan, and brought with him Adriano Galliani on one mission. To bring trophies back to San Siro.

And in summer 1987 along with the coming of Parma's manager Arrigo Sacchi (the man who later reformed the club), and Roma's midfielder Carlo Ancelotti, the club signed the Dutch star after a fierce competition with Real Madrid and Barcelona.

However Van Basten who didn't play much during his first year with the team because of the injury he had during the game against Lokomotive Leipzig, so he played only 19 games scoring 8 goals in them.

But 1988 wasn't the same, with Van Basten scoring 32 goals in his first full season, and helping Milan win their third European Cup, and the first since 1966, after scoring twice in a 4-0 win against Steaua Bucuresti in the final game in Camp Nou.

These 2 goals also made him the tournament's top scorer with 10 goals in 9 games, one of them was the famous 5-0 win for Milan against Real Madrid in San Siro.

The Year of 1990

In 1990; Van Basten, again, lead Milan to defeat Benfica 1-0 in the European Cup final, to secure the club's 4th title, and the second in a row.

In that season; he scored 24 goals in 40 games including a late penalty against FC Bayern in San Siro, a penalty that helped Milan qualify to the championship final.

But despite his great performance with Milan; Van Basten failed to win the World Cup with Netherlands, the European champion, despite being playing next to some of the best talents in the world including, Ruud Gullit, Ronald Koeman, and Frank Rijkaard.

They started with a disappointing performance in the group stage, with 3 consecutive draws against Egypt, England and Ireland respectively. They qualified to the next round as one of the best "thirds," to face West Germany in the second round, and lose 1-2.

Such performance had a negative effect on Marco who scored only 11 goals during his following season with Milan and spent most of the season in problems with Milan's manager Arrigo Sacchi.

Such conflict, plus failing to win the Serie A for the second time, forced Silvio Berlusconi to bring Fabio Capello to the managerial seat to bring Milan back to the picture.

And as if he gave them the kiss of life, Capello inspired Milan players and brought back the best in them and win 4 consecutive league titles, 3 super cups and one champions league title before leaving Milan to join Real Madrid in summer 1996.

Under Capello's eyes Van Basten made some of the best performances in his entire career scoring 49 goals in 60 games and helping the team reach another Champions league final against Olympic Marseille, however, suffering from 3 injuries - one of which against Marseille - caused Van Basten to spend his last 2 seasons with Milan in the hospital before officially retiring in summer 1995, at the age of thirty, as one of the best attackers in the history of soccer.

With The National Team

The prime of Van Basten's international career was in the year 1988 when he helped the Dutch team win their one and only major trophy in the 1988 European Championship (Euro 88) after defeating the Soviet Union 2-0 in the final game that witnessed Van Basten scoring one of the best goals in the history of soccer when he launched a volley from a dead angle in the 54th minute of the game.

Performance

Van Basten posed all the skills necessary to penalize any defense no matter how good they were. Just study his goal from the Euro 1988 against former Soviet union…

Great Vision

Marco Van Basten wasn't the type of players who would just shoot and try their luck, rather, he was one of the rare attackers in soccer who knew how and when to use their skills to make the best out of them.

I can go on and on about how smart he was, but this one moment summarizes his entire career. It was a beautiful goal he scored for AC Milan in San Siro.

That day, the ball was up in the air, and Van Basten was at the edge of the penalty area waiting to strike the ball once it comes down, however, it was almost impossible to score from that position because of the 3 defenders trying to block his way.

So what did he do?

Rather than shoot the ball towards the blocked goal, he hit the ball down, and made it jump off the ground, go above the 3 defenders and their goalkeeper and enter the goal.

He Was Fast Compared to His Size

The taller the attacker, the harder it becomes for him to rely on pace. Only a few who managed to improve their skills to move beyond the good header and the strong shot.

Carsten Jancker (1.93m) spent 23 years playing professional soccer and all his career goals were less than 100 goals, even though he played 6 consecutive years with Bayern Munich.

Being tall and strong is good but also has its limitations, probably not for Van Basten.

He was very fast compared to his physique. And this strength and physique enabled him to move beyond his role as an attacker. Sure he wasn't the fastest, but he developed the required pace to make dribbles, and move past defenders without much problems.

Excellent Shooting Skills With Both Feet

For me, the best play in Van Basten's career wasn't his goal against the Soviet Union in EURO 88, but the ball that hit the bar against Germany in 1992.

He was standing in front of the penalty area when he saw a header coming from Frank Rijkaard towards him. He took one step behind and with his right, non-dominant foot he struck the ball while standing on one foot.

The best thing about that shot wasn't the shot but rather, the technique. From his position, and from that distance, there was no way this ball won't go far above the German goal. At that time, no one in the soccer world produce this shot the same way Marco Van Basten did.

Alessandro Del Piero –

Pinturicchio

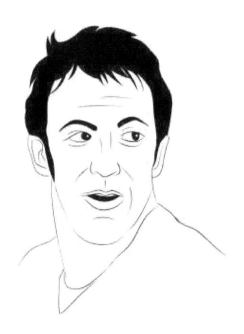

Full Name: Alessandro Del Piero

Date of birth: 9 November 1974

Nationality: Italian

Status: Retired (2014)

Clubs: Padova, Juventus (Italy) - Sydney FC (Australia) - Delhi Dynamos (India)

Goals scored and number of games: 343 goals in 868 games

Goals scored internationally: 27 in 91 Caps

Club Trophies:

- UEFA Champions League: 1995–96 (Juventus)
- UEFA Super Cup: 1996
- Italian League (Serie A): 6 Times 1994–95, 1996–97, 1997–98, 2001–02, 2002–03, 2004–05 (Juventus)
- Italian Cup 1994–95 (Juventus)
- Italian Super Cup: 4 Times (Juventus)

National Team Trophies:

- FIFA World Cup: Winner 2006
- Euro 2000: Silver Medalist

Personal Trophies:

- Italian Soccer of the Year: 1998, 2008
- Serie A-Top scorer: 2007–08
- FIFA's list of the greatest 100 soccerers of all times

Career Overview

Del Piero's relationship with the ball started when he started playing with his older brother who switched young Alessandro's position from a goalkeeper to the front line.

This was in 1982, six years before joining Padova in 1988, the team that witnessed his debut in the second division before a 13 million francs were offered to the club to let go of their best talent to Juventus in 1993.

A 19-Year Journey

Del Piero made his debut against Regina in 1993, the same year that witnessed him scoring 5 goals in 14 games before taking place the injured; Roberto Baggio and playing 50 games in the following season, scoring 11 goals and helping Juventus wins its 23rd league title and the first since the Platini era in the mid-80s.

This year 1994 was a successful year for Del Piero who helped Juventus reach the UEFA Cup final but Juventus lost to Parma 2-1 on aggregate before revenging themselves and defeating the same team, Parma, twice in the Italian cup final (2 legs) and again at the super cup final.

Such performance automatically got 21 year-old Del Pierro on the nomination list for the Ballon d'Or which he later lost to George Weah after coming fourth.

The following year , and after receiving Baggio's number-10 t-shirt, he helped Juventus add another European title to their cabinet after scoring twice in a 9-2 two-legged win against Paris Saint-Germain in the UEFA Super cup.

That cup was a good start for Del Piero who contributed to a combination of 67 goals, leading the Turin-based club to win the 1997 league titles and qualify to the Champions League final for the second time in a row.

However, Juventus lost the title to Ottmar Hitzfeld's Borussia Dortmund after a 3-1 defeat which witnessed Del Piero scoring Juve's only goal.

The next 3 years weren't successful for Del Piero and Juventus, though. The league champion finished seventh in 1999, and Carlo Ancellotti was hired to save the club after his success with Parma.

However, Del Piero's style didn't fit in the coach's tactic and it took the Italian player some time to adapt which affects his goal-scoring ratio, before things got worse, and his miserable season was topped with a set of injuries got him to play for no more than 8 games.

The best thing happening in the club though, was the signing of both David Trezeguet (from Monaco), and Pavel Nedved who came from Lazio to replace Zinedine Zidane who went to Madrid.

These two formed a fantastic trio with Del Piero who regained back his tenacity on the goal, scoring 45 goals and helping Juventus win 2 league titles, 2 super cups as well as reach the final game of the 2002-03 Champions League against Milan which, sadly for Del Piero, won on a penalty shootout.

2006, World cup, Calciopoli and Serie B

After helping Juve win their second league title in a row despite being benched for the team's new star, Zlatan Ibrahimović, Del Piero moved to Germany with the Italian team and scored the second goal in a late win against Germany in the semi-final game, before scoring a penalty kick against France in the final and securing Italy's 4th world cup title.

But things weren't that perfect back home, as Juventus was accused of assigning "specific" referees to manage their games in the famous scandal known by the name "Calciopoli" and the team was stripped from his last 2 league titles and forced to move to Serie B.

In one month, Del Piero watched his team getting ripped apart with important players like Gianluca Zambrotta, Fabio Cannavaro, Zlatan Ibrahimović and Patrick Vieira leave the team to compete elsewhere.

But he decided to not to leave and play along with Gianluigi Buffon, David Trezeguet and Pavel Nedved and made one of his best seasons, scoring 20 goals in 35 games and getting back to Serie A.

Yet, things were different now, and Juventus suffered for 5 consecutive years from Inter's dominance on the Italian soccer.

Between 2006 and 2011, the club has moved between 6 coaches who failed to win a single trophy. Del Piero now became older, and couldn't score as before, yet he still refused to leave his beloved Juventus until things get better which eventually happened with the coming of Del Piero's former teammate Antonio Conte as a new head manager in 2011.

That year, 2011-12, Juventus went on top of the league without a single defeat, with Del Piero appearing 3 times in 23 league appearances

In the 20th of May 2012, he played his last game against Napoli in the cup final to end his 19th year with the team in a great way before spending his last 3 years in soccer moving between Australia and India and doing the thing he knows best. Playing soccer

Performance

Although Del Piero was not the quickest, strongest and fastest striker, he still managed to score from nothing, especially when his team needed it most, which gave him that well-earned cult status.

Bend it like Del Piero

Only a few of players who had moves or goals named after them.

Ronaldo had the "Elastico," Jean-Pierre Papin's called his volleys he scored "Les Papinades," and Juve's created the "Gol alla Del Piero," since he had his own style in scoring goals.

He would start a move from the left of the penalty area with the ball at his possession, then – and here's the trick – use his left foot to move the ball away to create more space and give his right foot enough power and momentum to shoot the ball towards the opposite side of the goal.

He once did it against Empoli, he received a through ball as one-on-one with the goal keeper, and rather than approach the keeper and surpass him – or at least shoot from the inside – he sent a one-touched, bent ball towards the upper left side of the goalkeeper.

His other famous, a la Del Piero goal, was against Germany in the 2006 World Cup, but this time from inside the penalty area.

He received a back pass from Gilardino, and rather than dribble past the goalkeeper and send the ball nicely with his left foot, he bent his body and sent the ball with his right foot from a near-dead angle.

Pinturicchio and Little Baggio

One of Del Piero's nicknames among Juventus fans is Pinturicchio who was an Italian painter of the Renaissance. Pinturicchio was given that name, "The little painter" because of his small stature.

He was also the student of Rafaello Sanzio da Urbino (or Raphael), the famous Italian painter and architect of the High Renaissance.

Like Pinturicchio, Del Piero had both the small stature and the technical, artistic ability. And like Pinturicchio, Del Piero was the successor, and the best student, of Roberto Baggio, the master of all magic.

He had Baggio's dribbling skills, his courage, and his ability to spot weaknesses in the opponent's defense. And like Baggio, Del Piero was a free-kick master.

King of Free kicks

When you play in one team with Zinedine Zidane, and you be the one responsible for the free kicks then you must be so good.

That's how excellent Del Piero was with free kicks – especially the long ones. His technique was so simple, instead of hitting the ball with the inner side of his foot -The David Beckham way - he would use his bigger toe to hit the ball down up.

This way the ball goes up the wall then down towards the upper side of the goal, making it harder for the goalkeeper to catch it.

From the 290 goals he scored for Juventus in 19 years, Del Piero scored 42 free kicks (those that I managed to count) the majority of them were 30 plus yards away from the goal.

Ferenc Puskás - The Galloping Major

Full Name: Ferenc Puskás

Date of birth: 2 April 1927

Nationality: Hungarian & Spanish (Played for both countries)

Status: Died 17 November 2006

Clubs: Budapest Honvéd (Hungary) - Real Madrid (Spain)

Goals scored and number of games: 700 goals in 705 games

Goals scored internationally: 84 goals in 85 Caps

Club Trophies:

- UEFA Champions League: 3 times 1958–1959, 1959–1960, 1965–1966 (Real Madrid)
- Spanish League: 5 times 1960–61, 1961–62, 1962–63, 1963–64, 1964–65
- Hungarian League: 5 times 1949, 1950, 1952, 1954, 1955
- Spanish Cup (Copa del Rey): 1961–1962

Internationally:

- Olympic Gold Medalist: 1952
- FIFA World Cup Silver Medalist: 1954

Personal Trophies:

- Hungarian Player of the 20th century
- L'Equipe 's European player of the 20th century
- World Soccer Player of the Year: 1953
- European Player of the Year: 1953
- 1954 FIFA World Cup Golden Ball Winner
- Ballon d'Or: Second Place 1960
- Spanish League top scorer (El Pichichi): 4 times

Career Overview

Ferenc Puskás wasn't just a great player; he was also a legend who made his own mark in the history of soccer. Born in Budapest in 1927, Puskás started playing soccer at the age of 12 for a team called Budapest Honvéd in Hungary.

He then made his debut with the first team in 1943 to start a successful journey with the club and helping them win 5 league titles along with the other Hungarian legend and ex Barcelona player, Sandor Kocsis, who later faced Puskás in Spain and won 2 league titles with the Catalan club.

Internationally

2 years of development in Honvéd got Puskás a place in Tibor Gallowich's team and, in 1945, against Austria, Puskás played his first international game, helping Hungary win before later starting a winning strike of 33 consecutive wins one of which was a 2-0 win against Yugoslavia in the final match of the 1952 Olympics.

That day in Helsenki, he scored Hungary's first goal (and his 4th in the tournament) before assisting his teammate, Zoltán Czibor, to score the second two minutes before the end of the game.

Puskas also was part of the Hungarian team that thrashed England twice in only 7 months. The first, which was supposed to be a challenge between the Olympic champions and inventors of soccer, was played in 1953, in Wembley.

That day, November the 23rd, it took Nándor Hidegkuti less than 40 seconds to score the first goal for the Mighty Magyars, followed with another by the same player, and 2 consecutive goals by Puskas ending the first half with 4 goals to 2 before adding another 2 in the second half and end the game, and England's biggest all-time home defeat at a score of 6-3.

Another game was requested by the English who, hoping to revenge themselves, asked for a 7-months period to prepare however, what they thought should be their revenge turned to be a complete disaster.

They were 3 goals behind after only 19 minutes in the game that ended 7-1 for the Hungarian masters with 2 goals and 2 assists for Puskas who, also in the same year, helped Hungary win the Central European Championship (equivalent to the current Euro), after scoring 2 goals in Hungary's 3-0 win against Italy in Rome.

The 1954 World Cup

In the 1954 Swiss tournament; the Hungarian team played as if it came from another galaxy, scoring 17 goals in their first 2 games including a humiliating 8 goals win against West Germany in which Puskas has scored an opener (and his third in the tournament).

Mighty Magyars then both Brazil, and former champion, Uruguay with a score of 4-2 before facing the same German team they faced before in 4th of July, 1954 at the Wankdorf Stadium in Bern.

The game started with Puskas scoring an early opener only six minutes from the opening whistle, followed by a second from Zoltán Czibor however, the West Germans came from behind and equalized with 2 consecutive games.

Before doing what was later called "The Miracle of Bern," and securing the title with Helmut Rahn's late goal for the Germans six minutes before the end of the game to win the game despite Puskas's late equalizer that was cancelled by the referee.

About that day, Sir Alex Ferguson later said:

"He was a special player in his day without question. How that Hungary team didn't win the 1954 World Cup is beyond me."

Puskás and Real Madrid

After the Hungarian revolution in 1956, Puskás was about to sign for Manchester United who lost all his players in the famous Munich disaster however, his inability to speak English made him join Real Madrid instead.

And at the age of 31, Puskas formed one of the most memorable duos in the history of soccer with the Argentine legend, Alfredo Di Stefano.

Together, they scored 242 goals in 262 matches and won the champions league title 5 consecutive times in between 1961 and 1965.

Performance

Puskás was the striker that dominated the world of soccer for years and spread fear among countless of defenders that he played against.

The Booming Cannon

Even during the best days of his career, Ferenc Puskás wasn't the most athletic player around, not even close. He had a small tummy that grew with him.

In fact, he had a famous picture taken for him while playing against England with enough weight to put a normal soccer player on the bench for a year until he regains his fitness back, but yet, Puskás was a great soccer player, with a highly prestigious award named after him.

Why?

Because of his final touch, it was amazing.

Yes it's true, scoring goals was a lot easier back then they had 5 attacking players in all game tactics, still the most remarkable thing about Puskás was the missiles he sent with his left foot.

No matter where he stood, near the center or inside the six yards, all Puskás's shots screamed Power.

This is why he didn't care when the English called him *"The little fat chap"* prior to their game against Hungary in Wembley, the day when Puskás and his teammates caused the biggest home defeat to ever happen in the history of the land of hope and glory.

That day, 100,000 people watched Puskás score twice and make 2 assists, without even having to run.. It was all dependent on his eyes and his footwork.

In Hungary's second goal, he humiliated the English defense and created a space for himself right on the spot, before using all his power to hit the net. This was his key, no running, just picking the right place and using power and dribbling skills to score.

Puskás's second nickname – other than The Galloping Major – was The Booming Cannon. They gave him that name in Spain for his outstanding shooting power and accuracy.

Such power made him score 700 goals in 715, including with 84 goals in 85 international games with the Hungarian team which is until now considered one of the best international goal scoring records right after Gerd Muller who scored 68 goals for West Germany in 62 international games.

Dennis Bergkamp - The Iceman

Full Name: Dennis Nicolaas Maria Bergkamp
Date of birth: 10 May 1969
Nationality: Dutch
Status: Retired (2006)
Clubs: Ajax (Netherlannd) - Inter Milan (Italy) - Arsenal (England)
Goals scored and number of games: 309 goals in 820 games
Goals scored internationally: 37 goals in 79 Caps
Club Trophies:
- Europa league (UEFA Cup): Twice 1991–92 (Ajax) 1993–94 (Inter Milan)
- UEFA Cup Winners' Cup: 1986–87 (Ajax)
- English Premier League: 3 times 1997–98, 2001–02, 2003–04
- Dutch League (Eredivisie): 1989–90
- English Cup (FA Cup): 4 times
- Dutch Cup: Twice 1986–87, 1992–93
- English Super Cup (Community Shield): 3 times 1998, 2002, 2004

National team trophies:
- FIFA World Cup: Semi Final 1998

Personal trophies:
- Ballon d'Or: Second place
- FIFA World Player of the Year: Third place 1993 and 1997
- Dutch Soccer of the Year: Twice 1991 and 1992
- Euro 92 top scorer
- FIFA's greatest 100 soccerers of all times
- Arsenal's greatest 50 soccerers in history of the club (Second)

Career Overview

Dennis Bergkamp journey with soccer started in Amsterdam where he joined the academy of Ajax at the age of 12, six years before he became part of the team winning the European Cup Winners' Cup in 1987. Coached by the Ajax's legend, Johan Cruyff, Bergkamp played as a substitute in the final match against Lokomotive Leipzig.

The following year, Bergkamp was given more games to play following the departure of Van Basten to Milan. And in 32 appearances in all competitions, Bergkamp ended his second season as a pro with only 5 league goals and 7 assists.

Yet the best came eventually in 1990 when he lead Ajax to their first title since 84 scoring 13 league goals and 16 in all competitions to win the Dutch talent award and get his first international call against Italy, in September 1990, 3 months after the Netherland's terrible performance in the World Cup.

Between 1990 and 1993, a lot happened for Bergkamp since the day he was called to play for Netherlands.

Domestically, he scored 75 goals in 91 league games, putting him as the Eredivisie top scorer for 3 times in a row, before helping Luis Van Gaal's men win the 1992 UEFA Cup against Torino, the same year he won the golden boot with Netherlands in the European championship, from which they were eliminated after losing to Denmark (the champion) on penalties in the semi-final game.

All these, encouraged other European clubs to contact Ajax looking to sign Bergkamp who was approached by AC Milan's executives who gave him the chance to join their Dutch trio, Rijkaard, Gullit and Marco Van Basten.

But looking for a different challenge, he chose to stay away from such "comfortable" move and make his own adventure so he signed for Inter for 15 million dollars which made him the second most expensive player in the world.

In Inter, and though his first year with the team went well after helping the club win the 1994 UEFA Cup (and 25 goals in all competitions), it was hard for Bergkamp to adapt to life in Italy and its media that nominated him for the weekly "Donkey Award" multiple times.

Such hostile atmosphere caused his performance to decline, scoring only 5 goals in the 26 games he played for Inter in 1995, until he eventually approved on a 7.5 million- pounds deal with Arsenal which, despite finishing 12th in the league table the year before, offered Bergkamp the chance to discover himself again, and that exactly what happened.

With Arsenal, Bergkamp formed a fantastic duo with the star of the club back then, Ian Wright, and both helped the team finish fifth scoring a combination of 36 league goals.

The following year, Arsenal appointed Arsene Wenger to replace Bruce Rioch as the manager of the team.

With Wenger's attacking style, Bergkamp shined even more, and scored 22 times in Arsenal's first title win since 1989 to be a permanent member of the team between 1998 and 2006, winning 10 cups with the team, including their famous "Invincible" title in 2004.

Performance

Bergkamp was considered by many to be the most elegant striker ever existed. He could also look clumsy on the field, but as soon as he was close the the penalty box, he was highly effective at scoring

The Iceman: Cold Comfortable, and Classy

Only a few would hold their nerve, take a deep breath, and look at the ball before scoring a goal like the one Bergkamp scored in the last minute of the quarter final game against Argentina in 1998.

Known as "The Iceman," Bergkamp was one of the best players to stay calm under pressure. His famous goal against Leicester City says it all. In addition to the one, marvelous control he made over the ball, the way he made his final shot was remarkable.

He never seemed tense, not in this goal, or in other ones, such level of comfort while playing was his main theme throughout his career.

No matter how skilled they were, some of the best players in the world wouldn't dare to do tricks like the ones Bergkamp used to make, not because they lacked the skills, but when tension arises in the game, it's hard for a player to stay calm. Yet Bergkamp could.

When they asked him about how he frequently scored from overheads, he said:

The first option for any attacker is to drop the ball above the keeper's head. All keepers take a few steps to the front to secure both sides of the goal, and any smart player should use this to his advantage.

With no exaggeration, Dennis Bergkamp made the word "Class" stick to his name forever. Anyone born before 1995 would know this very well, regardless of their nationalities or what club they support. Bergkamp was more of an artist than a goal-scoring machine. He had his own philosophy, to score goals his own way.

Ever watched his goal against Newcastle United when he went past the defender with one marvelous move before scoring in Shay Given's net?

That was the way Bergkamp liked to score his goals. He made a hard move look so easy, yet when they asked him about his goal he said it was nothing, he has seen it in his mind and he know he would score this way.

Until today, Bergkamp is the only player in the history of the English league to score the best, the second best, and the third best goal of the month.

That was in August 1997, and the three goals were all scored in one game against Leicester City. He was a player who enjoyed soccer more than scoring goals.

In fact and, since 2000 and until he retired in 2006, the maximum number of goals Bergkamp scored with Arsenal in a single season was 14, yet he was indispensable because of the number of assists he gave to his teammates. In the 11 years Bergkamp spent with Arsenal, he scored 120 goals and made 116 assists.

The main that Bergkamp was chosen ahead of other Arsenal legends to be the second best player in the history of the Club - only behind Thierry Henry – was his ability to create chances out of absolutely nowhere.

One of the best goals to ever be scored against Gianluigi Buffon was the assist of Bergkamp when Arsenal met Juventus in the Champions League.

He was surrounded by two, then four defenders and with some excellent footwork; he tricked them all and passed the ball to Freddie Ljungberg who sent the ball over Buffon's head.

George Weah - The King George

Full Name: George Ousman Weah

Date of birth: 1 October 1966

Nationality: Liberian

Status: Retired (2007 after second comeback)

Clubs: Mighty Barrolle, Invincible Eleven (Liberia) - Africa Sports, Tonnerre Yaoundé (Ivory Coast) - Monaco, Paris Saint-Germain, Marseille (France) - AC Milan (Italy) - Chelsea, Manchester City (England) - Al Jazira (UAE)

Goals scored and number of games: 274 goals in 599 games

Goals scored internationally: 22 goals in 60 Caps

Club trophies:

- Italian League (Serie A): Twice 1995–96, 1998–9 (Milan)
- French League (League 1): 1993–94 (PSG)
- English Cup (FA Cup): 1999–2000 (Chelsea)
- French Cup: 3 Times 1991 (Monaco), 1992–93, 1994–95 (PSG)
- French League Cup: 1995 (PSG)

National team trophies:

None

Personal trophies:

- Ballon d'Or: 1995
- Onze d'Or: 1995
- FIFA World Player of the Year: 1995
- UEFA Champions League Top Scorer: 1994–95
- African Soccerer of the Year: 3 Times 1989, 1994, 1995
- The 100 Greatest Soccerers of All Time by World Soccer magazine

Career Overview

Weah started his career in Liberia playing for a local youth team called Young Survivors for which he played for 3 years in a row before making his first impact as young player in 1987 after scoring 24 goals in 23 games with his Liberian-based club, "Invincible Eleven".

Later, this club which later became Weah's gate to join two of the biggest clubs in Africa, Africa Sport and Tonnerre Yaoundé. After doing fine with the former two, Weah was asked to do trials for AS Monaco and train under the eyes of Monaco's manager at that time, Arsene Wenger who, known for giving opportunities to young talents, immediately admired Weah, and offered him a deal in 1988.

In Monaco; Weah started his journey scoring 23 goals during his first 38 games; followed by 26 goals in the next 2 seasons before helping the team win the French Cup on his last year with Moncao (1991-92).

That year he scored 23 goals in 47 games before leaving to Paris to join Paris Saint-Germain and help them win 4 trophies; including the league title in 1993-94.

1995 and The Ballon d'Or

In the year 1995, Weah became the only player in soccer history to win the best player in Africa, Europe and the World in one year after his fantastic season with PSG.

That year, Weah made some fantastic performances and lead PSG to the semifinal of the Champions League despite the fact that the French team couldn't, at that time, compete with giants like Barcelona, Real Madrid, Juventus, Milan and Bayern Munich in both; money and quality of players. Weah was also the top scorer of the tournament with 7 goals.

In 1995; PSG was all about Weah and his French teammate Youri Djorkaeff.

Weah was literally doing everything on the field, from assisting his teammates to scoring wonderful, solo goals like his famous goal against Bayern Munich in Alianz Arena. All that made Weah one of the few who managed to win both the Ballon d'OR and Onze d'OR in one year and the only African to become the best soccer player in the world.

The Next Van Basten

After suffering from a set of injuries in 1993 that later lead to his retirement, AC Milan had to search for someone to substitute Marco Van Basten, and they found what they need in Weah.

In Milan, Weah helped the team win the Serie A in his first season with the club after scoring 15 goals, including an amazing league goal against Verona in November 8th 1996 when he received the ball inside Milan's penalty area and went along through 6 defenders before scoring a Maradona-type goal.

He then won his second league title with Milan in 1999 before moving in summer 1999 to Chelsea with which he won the FA Cup before leaving in the next year to Manchester City and scoring 4 goals in 9 games before leaving them in the January to join Olympic Marseille until the end of the season moving to Abu Dhabi to play for Al Jazira until he retired in summer 2003.

Performance

He had the speed of an Olympic sprinter and few defenders in the world could compete with that…

The modern attacker

The reason why Weah won the Ballon d'Or is still mysterious for many who didn't know a lot about Weah or watch him play. Weah didn't play for a strong national team, and amongst famous African players, Weah has won than any of Drogba or Samuel Eto'o.

During the early 90s, Weah, who came before both Romario and Ronaldo - was revolutionary. Doing the stuff we now cheer for anytime we see players like Ronaldo or Messi do, but without being surrounded by another two to complete his MSN or BBC.

Weah was better than most of his peers at the way he quickly used his feet. Some great players are lefties, others prefer completely using the right foot like Thierry Henry, but Weah could do exactly what he was good at using any of his feet. Whatever foot was available would do the job.

Super Powerful

Not just that. Physically, Weah, was Europe's best player to combine between both power and speed. His style with the ball was quite similar to that of Eusebio, not because they were both African descendents, but because each one of them had great speed and great power. Eusebio was called the Black Panther, and Weah was the Black Lion.

He had enough speed to move the ball past two or three defenders, run from behind and all of a sudden he's one-on-one against the keeper.

He once, while playing for Milan, received the ball inside his penalty area, ran along the whole field, dribbling back and forth through 4 defenders and scoring. That was only 5 minutes before the final whistle when everybody is sore and out of breath.

It was almost impossible for a defender to stop Weah once he goes past him. The speed and the sheer power he had were from somewhere else.

He had more than excellent shooting power. That was shown in his goal against Bayern Munich in Germany while playing for Paris Saint-Germain.

Surrounded by six German defenders, and without lots of space to create enough shooting power, he fired a bullet towards Oliver Kahn's net.

Romario - Baixinho (The Short One)

Full Name: Romário de Souza Faria
Date of birth: 29 January 1966
Nationality: Brazilian
Status: Retired in 2009
Clubs: Vasco da Gama, Flamengo, Fluminense (Brazil) - PSV Eindhoven (Netherland) - Barcelona, Valencia (Spain) - Al Sadd (Qatar) - Miami FC (USA) - Adelaide United (Australia)
Goals scored and number of games: 743 goals in 956 games
Goals scored internationally: 55 goals in 70 Caps
Club trophies:
- The Dutch league (With Eindhoven): 3 times (1989, 1991 and 1992)
- The Dutch Super cup (With Eindhoven): 1 time (1992)
- Spanish league (With Barcelona): 1 time (1993-1994)
- Qatar League Cup (With Al – Saad): 1 time (2003-2004)

National team trophies:
- FIFA World Cup: 1 time (1994)
- FIFA Confederations Cup 1997
- Copa América: 1989, 1997

Personal trophies:
- FIFA World Cup Golden Ball: 1994
- Onze d'Or: 1994 (awarded by Onze Magazine for the best player in Europe)
- FIFA World Player of the Year: 1994
- Dutch Soccerer of the Year: 1989
- Top scorer for the UEFA Champions League: 1989–90, 1992–93

- Dutch League's top scorer: 1998-89, 1989–1990, 1990–91
- FIFA World Player of the Year – Runner Up
- Brazilian league's top scorer: 2000, 2001, 2005
- Top scorer in the 1988 Seoul Summer Olympics (and silver medalist)
- FIFA Confederations Cup Top Scorer: 1997
- Club's Player of the Year (Vasco da Gama): 1987, 1988, 2000, 2001
- Marca World Cups All-Time Team: 2014 (By the famous Spanish newspaper "Marca")

Career Overview

Romario started his journey with soccer at the age of 15 when he played for a small team in Rio de Janeiro called Olaria after being rejected by his favorite club, Vasco da Gama, for what they called, lacking proper physique for an attacker."

This was changed, however, 2 years later when he approached them again at Vasco and convinced them with his skills.

And at the age of 19, Romario made his debut with Vasco, scoring 11 goals in 21 league games and helping them win the regional league (Campeonato Carioca) in 1987 before doing it again the following year but this time with 20 goals in 25 games.

Now being the best player in Rio de Janeiro (1987 - 1988), Romario was called for his international debut with the Brazilian team heading to Seoul for the Olympic Games.

And despite losing the gold medal to the Soviet Union, Romario won the golden boot for the 7 goals he scored in the tournament, including the opener he scored in the final.

The following summer, Romario started his journey in Europe playing for PSV Eindhoven.

The club was having 2 glorifying years and needed reinforcement to add depth to their front line which they found in Romario who, forming a strong duo with Wim Kieft, scored 19 goals in 24 league games and helped Guus Hiddink and his men win their 3rd league title in a row.

The next year however, was time to focus on the national team, and at the age of 24, Romario made his first real impact with Brazil in the 1989 Copa America.

Despite failing to score at any of Brazil's 4 group-stage games, Romario amazed everyone during the second round, scoring in each of the following 3 games against Argentina, Paraguay, and Uruguay in front of 150,000 raving Brazilian fans gathered in the famous Maracanã stadium in Rio de Janeiro.

Romario then spent 3 more years with PSV, winning 2 more league titles, 3 Dutch cups, 3 golden boots and the second place in the FIFA 1993 Player Award.

F.C Barcelona

One year before the World Cup, and right after his success in Netherlands, Barcelona signed Romario to become part of Johan Cruyff's dream team alongside players like Pep Guardiola, Hristo Stoichkov and Michael Laudrup.

That year, Romario made his best performance ever, scoring 30 league games, including a hat-trick against Real Madrid in a 5-0 win in Camp Nou.

Cruyff's dream team kept their impressive performance in the Champions League and reached the final against AC Milan and, despite being widely nominated to grab an easy win, Barcelona lost the title in a 4-0 win for Milan who won their 5th title.

But it wasn't all bad for Romario, who flew to the United States to compete with Brazil in the World Cup they haven't won since 1970.

With an impressive performance alongside his partner, Bebeto, Brazil won their 4th cup title with Romario being chosen as the best player in the world for his impressive performance both domestically, and internationally.

From Catalonia to Brazil

After returning from USA, things escalated between Cruyff and the undisciplined Romario who terminated his contract and took off to Brazil to join Flamengo only 13 games from the beginning of the 1994-95 season.

With Flamengo though, Romario was the league's top scorer twice and won 2 consecutive league titles with the team yet, he still wanted to play in Europe so he flew to Spain in summer 1996 to play for Valencia.

However, a clash between him and the team's coach at that time, Luis Aragones, forced him to pack his stuff again and move back to Brazil after scoring 4 goals in only 5 league games with Valencia.

Now coming back to Flamengo, Romario scored 35 goals in 36 games to get a call from Brazil's coach, Mário Zagallo, to be part of the team defending its world title in France 1998. However, and with tears in his eyes, Romario was injured only 2 days before the beginning of the tournament and had to watch the Brazilian team get smashed against France in the championship final.

He then kept his great performance with Flamengo the following year, scoring 46 goals in 54 games however, being seen partying the night after Flamengo was knocked out from the cup's quarter-final game ended his days in Flamengo.

He decided to move back with Vasco and score a remarkable number of 122 goals in 135 games that helped them win 4 titles in 3 years including Vasco's 4th league title and the last one since then.

The 1000's goal

Since he last won the league title with Vasco in 2000, Romario moved a lot between teams (8 moves between clubs between 2000 and 2007).

However, the highlight of this period was on May 2007, when Romario scored a penalty against Sport Recife to net the goal number 1000 in his career which put him among a handful of players who ever managed to score this huge number of goals.

Performance

Romario was a great player, but what was so great about him was his ability to even raise him higher in the skies. This caused a fear among many defenders which gave him an unfair advantage on the soccer field.

Confidence

Romario's extreme confidence and lack of modesty - to the extent of calling himself the second greatest player of all times - makes him unique both personally and professionally.

Despite the fact that cockiness is not admired in some societies, Romario's deep sense of self-worth and importance that stemmed from his strong work ethic helped him become the legend people talk about.

This may sound insane, and arrogant, but at the end of the day a hard working attacker very sure of himself is far better than a very skilled one but full of doubts.

Like I previously mentioned, the attacking style or role introduced by Romario and George Weah was new to soccer back in the 80s and early 90s. The attacker who runs along the entire field, dribbling past 3,4, or even 5 players wasn't yet available.

That role was only exclusive to the best of playmakers and attacking midfielders like Maradona and sometimes Platini,

Back then, the only job a classic center forward had was stick to the penalty area and try to finish properly, and it did require a deep sense of courage and self-assurance to be deeply rooted inside the forward's mind to carry on these new duties. And Romario had such mentality.

The huge confidence he had inspired his dribbling skills. A dribble is more than just an attempt to move past a couple of defenders, it's more of a mental challenge between one soldier and an army. In order to win, the soldier must be both risky and self-assured.

Romario's confidence in his abilities made him magnificent under pressure. Any time he faced the goalkeeper, he was neither rushed nor slow.

He had what Thierry Henry calls it, the freeze point, when an attacker pause his move for a sector of a second to assess the situation and distract the goalkeeper who will naturally have to break his momentum and stop midways to guess the attackers next move.

In one game while playing for Barcelona, he received a cross inside the penalty area.

And rather than directly shoot the ball, he assisted himself with a back-heel, to get rid of the defender coming from behind before bending his body and firing the ball towards the net.

I have watched plenty of soccer, and not too many players will do the same thing. It requires confidence and trust in one's ability to score.

Heading Skills

Romario (1.67m) had more headers scored than Jan Koller, the 2.02m Czech attacker who played for Dortmund in the early 2000s. He could literally score from anywhere inside the box with his head regardless of the size of the defender marking him or where he stands inside the penalty area.

The key to this was his excellent positioning and shot accuracy, he didn't rely on power but rather the point at which he should target the ball away from the goalkeeper. This helped him score a lot of goals when the goalkeeper failed to reach the ball despite taking the right position inside the goal area.

King of Chips

Also Romario was literally, a chip-over king. Inside the area, Romario made sending the ball above the keeper's head something ordinary.

It seemed like he was challenging himself rather than try to score a goal.

For instance, in one of his games with PSV, he was in a counter attack near the left wing, with only one defender behind him, and rather than moving inside the penalty area and shoot from an easier spot, he sent a long ball above the keeper's head.

The keeper wasn't way too far from his goal, but being unpredictable is what made Romario score.

Once again against Chile in Copa America 97, Ronaldo passed him the ball near the edge of the penalty area and rather than pass to one of 3 teammates taking better positions –including Rivaldo - he chose to go deep inside the penalty despite being surrounded by 4 Chilean defenders and he scored an excellent chip-over.

Ian Rush – The Ghost

Full Name: Ian James Rush

Date of birth: 20 October 1961

Nationality: Welsh

Status: Retired (2000)

Clubs: Chester City, Liverpool, Leeds United, Newcastle United, Sheffield United, Wrexham - Juventus (Italy) - Sydney Olympic (Australia)

Goals scored and number of games: 411 goals in 905 games

Goals scored internationally: 28 goals in 73 Caps

Club trophies:

- UEFA Champions League: Twice 1980–81, 1983–84 (Liverpool)
- English League: 5 Times 1981–82, 1982–83, 1983–84, 1985–86, 1989–90 (Liverpool)
- English Cup (FA Cup): 3 Times 1985–86, 1988–89, 1991–92 (Liverpool)
- English League Cup: 5 Times 1980–81, 1981–82, 1982–83, 1983–84, 1994–95 (Liverpool)
- English Super Cup (Community Shield): 3 Times 1982, 1986, 1990 (Liverpool)

National team trophies:

None

Personal trophies:

- Liverpool's goal scorer of all times (346 goals in 660 games)
- Wales all time goal scorer (28 goals in 73 games)

Career Overview

18 September 1976 Ian Rush; known for his famous mustache is the historical attacker of Liverpool soccer club scoring 346 goals in 660 games during the 15 years that he spent with the English team.

Rush who was unlucky to be born in Wales, started his career in Chester City in 1978 before grabbing Liverpool's attention with the 17 goals he scored with Chester in 1979 which made them approach him with an offer that made him the most expensive youngster at that time

In his first year with Liverpool; the 19 year old kid failed to score in any of his 9 appearances in but in the following year he showed everybody what he's got after scoring 30 goals in 49 games and helping the team win the league title after losing it to Aston Villa the year before.

The following two seasons were even better for Rush who won the PFA young player of the year after scoring 24 league goals that helped Liverpool win their second league title in a row before scoring 47 goals in 65 in the 1983-84 season.

This made him win the European golden boot after helping the Reds win their third consecutive league title and their fourth European cup (Champions league) after defeating A.S Roma in the final game.

He then spent 3 other seasons with Liverpool, scoring 99 goals in 157 games and helping the team add another league title to their trophy cabinet before he decided to leave to Italy and join Juventus in summer 1986.

After playing for a year on loan with Liverpool, Rush finally arrived to Turin to start his journey with Juventus in summer 1987 however failing to settle in Turin and failing to keep up with the Italian defensive style made him only score 7 goals in 29 league appearances as well as 2 goals in the European cup so he decided to return back to Liverpool the next summer.

And in May 1989; Rush was about to celebrate his fifth league title in Anfield however; a sudden 90 minute goal by Michael Thomas (who later played for Liverpool) made Arsenal win their ninth title and prevent Liverpool from winning the double (the league and the FA cup).

However, in the following year, Rush helped the Reds win their 18th and last league title after scoring 26 goals in 48 matches including 18 goals in 36 league appearances.

1996 and Retirement

At 35, Rush decided that it's time to leave Liverpool after scoring 7 goals in his last season with the team so he joined Leeds United in 1996 before joining Newcastle in the following year to play next to Alan Shearer and in 2000; Rush retired from soccer after spending his last year playing for Sydney Olympic in the Australian league.

Performance

Rush was not the best dribbler, not the fastest striker, not even the strongest one, but he was without doubts one of the most clever and smartest one's.

One Step Ahead

The older I grew, the more I realized how stupid I was for hating Ian Rush. I still don't know why I didn't like him when I was a kind, probably for the mustache, or maybe because he cared only for scoring goals

Young soccer fans – like me back then – love to see some style every now and then. As I grew older I realized that it's all about how many goals a player scores not how did he score them. And that's how I became a fan of Ian Rush.

Rush was classical attacker, more of the Shearer-type than the Ronaldo-type, and had a sharp finishing skills like none of his peers. He's Liverpool's top goal scorer of all times with 346 in his pocket.

But despite his strong finish or his nicely aimed headers, Rush's key strength in my opinion was the way he moved between the two central backs playing against him.

I recall two of his goals against Everton in the Goodison Park Stadium. This was a game when Everton was a real contender.

(Side note: Everton has 9 league titles, that's Chelsea and Manchester City's titles combined).

During this game, Rush scored two goals, they were both the same, they were both technically brilliant, and they both were about the same trick from Rush.

He would stick his eyes on Liverpool's right winger – I don't know whom he was, but he assisted the two goals – and once this winger receives the ball, Rush would take position between the two center backs and await for the cross to move diagonally and meet the ball.

Such move allows him to sneak behind the first defender (the one standing in front of Rush) and be one step ahead the second defender (the one standing behind him).

Excellent header

This is why he thrived in English soccer in the 80s. Back then in England, the whole soccer game was about throwing long balls to the front and seeing what happens.

It was the same classic defensive English soccer played since the 50s, there weren't teams playing attacking soccer like Arsenal and Manchester City nowadays (ironically Arsenal was named Boring Arsenal because of his defensive style). To shine in England at that time, being excellent at air plays was a must. And here where Ian Rush excelled the best.

He wasn't super tall (Rush was only 1.8 m), but his positioning, combined with his jumping and heading techniques were amazing and enabled him of scoring lots of goals for Liverpool.

Didier Drogba – The Tito

Full Name: Didier Yves Drogba Tébily

Date of birth: 11 March 1978

Nationality: Ivorian

Status: Currently playing for Montreal Impact (MLS)

Clubs: Le Mans, Guingamp, Marseille (France) - Chelsea (England) - Shanghai Shenhua (China) - Galatasaray (Turkey) - Montreal Impact (Canada)

Goals scored and number of games: 338 goals in 740 games

Goals scored internationally: 63 goals in 104 Caps

Club trophies:
- UEFA Champions League: 2012-12 (Chelsea)
- English Premier League: 4 Times
- Turkish League: Once
- English Cup (FA Cup): 4 Times
- Turkish Cup: Once
- English League Cup: 3 Times
- English Super Cup (Community Shield): Twice
- Turkish Super Cup: Once

National team trophies:
None

Personal trophies:
- Onze d'Or: Once 2004
- African Soccer of the Year: Twice (2006, and 2009)
- English soccer of the year: Twice
- French soccer of the year: Once
- Turkish Soccer of the Year: Once
- Ivory Coast Player of the Year: 3 Times
- Premier League Top Scorer: Twice

Career Overview

Born in Abidjan, Drogba moved to Paris in 1993 with his parents in after they both were laid from their jobs. Drogba, now at the age of 15, started playing for some local teams before joining Levallois.

This team whose stadium's name was later changed to "Stade Didier Drogba" after their Ivorian player who made his first youth impact wearing their yellow shirt.

Drogba then joined Le Manc in 1997 however, suffering from injury problems, it took him four years to establish himself as a player and find himself a place in the first team and in 2001.

That year he became the team's main attacker and scored 24 appearances in the League2 which lured Guingamp, the club struggling in the first division, to buy him in the January transfer window.

The plan was to help them not to relegate which is exactly what happened as the team finished 16th, only 2 points above Metz, thanks to Drogba's 3 goals and 4 assists in the 11 games he played with the club in 2002.

Things changed however in 2003 as Drgoba finally established himself as a world class attacker scoring 21 goals that helped Guingamp not just avoid relegation, but qualify to the European championships after finishing 7th on the league table above famous teams like Lille and Paris Saint-Germaine.

Such performance, grabbed the attention of Marseille whose people watched Drgoba carefully during his year and half spell with Guingamp so they signed him in summer 2003 to help them with his 32 goals to make a fantastic season.

The team, despite dropping from 3rd to 7th on the league table, reached the UEFA Cup final game thanks to Drogba's 11 European goals that year. However, they lost the title 2-0 to Valencia in a game where Drogba played despite being seriously injured one week before it started.

Making history at Chelsea

With the departure of Claudio Ranieri and the club's leading scorer Jimmy Floyd Hasselbaink in 2004, Chelsea, with their new manager Jose Mourinho, needed to fill the gap at their front side and bring someone to compete with Eidur Gudjohnsen and they found what they need in Drogba for a fee of $ 34 million dollars.

However, despite looking promising, Drogba's first days with Chelsea weren't as bright as everyone in the club wanted them to be. He was still adapting to the atmosphere in England and was absent for 8 weeks because of a serious injury in his abdominal muscles.

However, things started to change gradually as he scored a winner against Liverpool in the League cup before helping the Blues finish on top of the league for the second time in their history, and the first time in 50 years.

The following year 2006 was a very successful year for Drogba, both domestically and internationally.

He started the season by scoring twice against Arsenal in the English super cup (the Community Shield) before helping the Ivorian team to qualify to the World Cup for the first time in their history after eliminating both Cameroon and Egypt from the qualification.

He then scored a winner against Nigeria to help Ivory Cost qualify to the final game of the African cup of nations for the first time in 25 before losing to Egypt on penalties. He then continued his successful season by adding a second league title to Chelsea's cabinet.

That year, Drogba established himself as Chelsea's number one attacker and the first choice for Mourinho. Unfortunately, the departure of the Portuguese coach, and a set of successive injuries and bans affected his performance in 2007 and 2008, scoring only 13 goals in the 2 English leagues that went to Manchester United.

Yet he soon regained his form back in 2009, scoring 29 league goals that helped him both win the league medal for the third time, and the premier league's golden boot for the second time since 2006.

Allianz Arena 2012

Everything Drogba did for Chelsea couldn't be compared with what he did that night on the 19th of May 2012.

For the second time in the club's history, Chelsea became one step away from winning their first ever Champions league title and one step away from becoming the only club in the city to win the European cup and declaring themselves as "The New Pride of London."

Unfortunately Chelsea was about to face the former runner-up, Bayern Munich, and where? On Bayern's stadium, Allianz Arena.

Chelsea spent the entire season off form, and things got worse when their 2 key defenders, Branislav Ivanović and the captain John Terry received cards during the semi-final game against Barcelona, and were both prevented from attending the final.

The game were almost one-sided, with Petr Cech doing a heroic performance under Chelsea's 3 bars and saving more than 6 clear chances for Bayern which eventually scored, by Thomas Muller, only 7 minutes before the end of the second half.

Desperate for a quick equalizer, Chelsea's players went all-attack and on the 88th minute one man stepped up with an amazing outside-in header after receiving Juan Mata's corner.

The game then went to a penalty shootout which was again ended by Drogba scoring the final penalty for Chelsea to finally put "The Blues" on the winning list of the European Champions League.

China, Turkey, and Chelsea again

Drogba left Chelsea a week after the game against Bayern, looking for a new challenge in Shanghai Shenhua however, feeling he still have more to give got him to cut his contract a year later and fly to Istanbul and play for Galatasaray, the only Turkish team to ever win a major European championship.

With his new club, Drogba proved himself as a winning deal as he helped Galatasaray win three domestic titles and was chosen the Turkish soccerer of the year in 2013.

He then returned back to Chelsea to play one more season under the returned-hero, Jose Mourinho and finished his final season at London with his fourth, and last, league title.

Performance

Drogba was a complete attacker and a Premier League legend, not just for the titles he won for Chelsea, but also because he had all the qualities any coach dreams of.

Head of Gold

In the late 90s, Chelsea had a 1.93 m Norwegian player called Tore André Flo who scored 23 out of his 50 Chelsea goals from headers and crossed balls.

Flo wasn't a superstar attacker, but when he left in 2000, everybody in Chelsea knew it won't be easy to find someone better than him in air plays….Until they signed Drogba.

Drogba, who scored 22% of his Chelsea goals from headers (37 headers from a total of 164 without counting crosses scored by foot,) was an artist in taking positions and beating defenders in air plays.

He was the type of players who didn't need much space for himself to jump or build enough power to shoot. Also he was one of the best in using his body against opposite defenders.

That equalizer one minute before the final whistle against Bayern Munich in the Champions League final was the highlight of Drogba's career.

It was a corner, all Bayern's players were inside their penalty and he couldn't position himself inside the six-yards' area, so rather than stick to the crowd, he took two steps forward, put himself in a position that wasn't perfect for playing a header - but it was the best he could get – and sent a strong, curvy header from outside in and gave Chelsea the kiss of life.

Excellent Shooting Quality with Both Feet

By nature, Drogba is a player who excels better inside the penalty area, yet his shooting skills were remarkable and gave him the ability to turn tiniest of opportunities into sugar.

His 2 wonderful goals against Liverpool and Barcelona sum it all, and the two were scored from a tough position, outside the penalty area and with two different foot.

Against Liverpool he controlled the ball with his chest, rotated and struck the ball as hard as he could with his left foot and left Pepe Reina watching the ball while it entered his goal.

A few weeks later, the same scenario was repeated in the Champions League, but this time with his right, non-dominant foot against Vicrot Valdes. In both goals, against both teams, the quality of Drogba's shot was excellent, and didn't change by changing feet.

This goal was again repeated a few weeks later against Everton. Drogba received the ball alone, with his back to the goal, and surrounded by two defenders. What did he do? He rotated, dropped the ball onto the ground, and from at least 37 yards he sent a marvelous shot that kept Everton's keeper, Tim Howard, mystified.

A Spot Master

Drogba developed his skills at Chelsea to include not only headers and long shots, but free kicks.

Not long after he came to Chelsea, he made himself the number two free-kick taker in the team, right after Frank Lampard, because of his a-la-Ronaldo free kick style.

From the spot, Drogba scored for Chelsea by flicking the ball down up like Cristiano Ronaldo. He did it first against Wigan, then continued to do it again, scoring 13 free kicks for Chelsea in addition to a dozen more of penalties.

Marcelo Salas - El Matador

Full Name: José Marcelo Salas Melinao
Date of birth: 24 December 1974
Nationality: Chilean
Status: Retired (2008)
Clubs:Universidad de Chile (Chile) - River Plate (Aregentina) - Lazio, Juventus (Italy)
Goals scored and number of games: 285 goals in 523 games
Goals scored internationally: 37 goals in 70 Caps
Club trophies:
-   UEFA Cup Winners' Cup: 1998–99 (Lazio),
-   UEFA Super Cup: 1999 (Lazio)
-   Italian League (Serie A): 1999–2000 (Lazio), 2001–02, 2002–03 (Juventus)
-   Italian Cup (Coppa Italia): 1999–2000 (Lazio)
-   Italian Super Cup: 3 times 1998, 2000 (Lazio) , 2002 (Juventus)
-   Argentine Premier Division: Twice
-   Chilean Premier Division: 1994, 1995
-   SuperCopa Libertadores (River Plate)

National team trophies:
None
Personal trophies:
-   FIFA World Cup Bronze Shoe: 1998

Career Overview

Marcelo Salas started his career in 1989 at the youth team of his local team, Deportes Temuco FC.

However, his father, a soccer coach himself, took his son to Santiago hoping he could get the later to join Universidad de Chile, the country's second most successful club in 1992.

During his first year in Universidad, Salas failed to score more than one goal in 15 league appearance.

However, the following year, 1994 was totally different for the 20 years old kid who literally exploded, scoring 41 goals in 46 games, and helping the club break Colo-Colo's domination over the Chilean soccer and winning its first league title since 1969.

The following year, Salas added another league medal to his trophy room, scoring 17 goals in 27 league games.

He then lead the club's campaign to win its first ever Copa Libertadores title, scoring 4 goals in 10 games however, Universidad's hopes were cut short after losing the second semi-final leg against River Plater despite Salas's equalizer in the first one.

But since every cloud has a silver lining, Salas's performance grabbed the attention of River Plate's executives who were in the market for a striker after the expected departure of their attacking star Hernan Crespo who left the club to join Parma.

In summer 1996, Salas was first introduced to the public, as River Plate's first signing of the year.

River Plate

In his first season in Argentina; Salas scored 11 league goals, helping River Plate win both the opening league, the Apertura, and the closing league, the Clausura titles as well as the Supercopa Sudamericana; a championship only for past winners of the Copa Libertadores.

He then scored 20 goals during his second, and last, year with River Plate, helping them add another Clausura title before flying to Italy to start his journey in Europe, precisely in Lazio.

Lazio and Winning Everything

In Lazio, Salas become part of the historical Lazio team that had some of the world's best young talents of that time, including legends like Alessandro Nesta, Pavel Nedved, Sinisa Mihajlovic, Dejan Stankovic, Juan Sebastian Veron, Christian Vieri, Atlético Madrid 's current coach, Diego Simeone.

Between the years of 1998 and 2000, Salas made history with Lazio, scoring48 goals for the team, and helping them win its first, and only, European championship, after defeating Real Mallorca in the 1999 Cup Winners' Cup final.

He then followed up by another one after a tough win against Manchester United in the UEFA Super cup before winning Lazio's second league title, and the first in 26 years, with only 1 point above Juventus in the 1999-2000 season.

Juventus, Injuries and, River Plate

In 2001; and after seeing most of his teammates move to bigger clubs; Salas followed his Czech teammate; Pavel Nedved and signed for Juventus in a huge deal of 25 million Euros.

However, a set of serious injuries forced the Chilean attacker to spend most of his journey in Torino injured; appearing only in 11 games during his first season with the team before securing a loan move back to River Plate that was transformed into a long term contract with the Argentine club in 2004.

Yet, In Argentina, Salas failed to regain back his form after another set of injuries that caused to think about retiring after scoring only 17 goals in his 43 appearances with the team, including a semi- final defeat against Sao Paolo in Copa Libertadoras.

Feeling his days in soccer were limited, Salas decided to move back to Chile and join his beloved, Universidad, with which he scored 37 goals before announcing his retirement in 2008.

Performance

Although the was not tall, Salas was a true heading master, and he could easily beat taller and more powerful defenders.

El Matador: A bullfighter

Early, after his first few games with Chile, Salas was nicknamed "El Matador" for his speed, strong physique and attitude of impulsiveness that showed itself with every fight on the ball and every shot he took.

His style was quite similar to Alexis Sanchez, aggressive on the ball, hungry to score more, and a winning mentality that doesn't give up. Such aggressiveness showed itself even while shooting penalties.

Salas penalty-taking style was also aggressive, he rarely tried to bluff the goalkeeper, all he had to do was run as far as he could, and shoot the ball with as much power as he could. It was power written all over his face.

He was also the type of player who didn't wait on the ball so much, the decision to shoot was the first to come to Salas's mind regardless of the position he took or where the ball was.

For him it was just aim and fire, supported by his short, yet strong, body (1.73m) that allowed him to shoot without a little need for preparation. He would shoot from a small hole, and the ball will come out with the right speed and the right power, just like the goal he scored against Torino in the Seirie A.

He went for the ball, tackled one of Torino's defenders inside the penalty area, and while being on the ground, with no space and no momentum whatsoever, he sent bullet that hit right on top of the keeper's left arm.

Only a handful of players who could use such limited space to create strong shots, exactly like his other goal against Liga de Quito in Copa Libertadores.

He received a long ball, assisted himself with his right foot, and without waiting, he pulled off a stunner with the left one.

At any given moment, Salas would risk getting injured for a goal.

Il Grinta is a word the Italians use to describe the determined, aggressive, passionate type of soccer they play in Italy, and it's the best word I can use to describe Salas's performance on the field, determined, aggressive and passionate to the extent that he could risk getting injured for the ball.

This may sound reckless, however, nothing bothers a defender than a highly skilled attacker who doesn't stop moving and fights for every ball.

Like Ivan Zamorano, Salas's style depended mostly on scaring defenders from getting injured themselves, he was willing to collide in the air or raise his foot up too high, thus forcing the defender to keep away in order to stay safe.

This helped Salas score many headers, only depending on the defenders willingness to back off to avoid getting hit by the Chilean attacker.

Jean-Pierre Papin - JPP

Full Name: Jean-Pierre Papin

Date of birth: 5 November 1963

Nationality: France

Status: Retired (2001)

Clubs: Valenciennes, Marseille, Bordeaux, Guingamp (France) - Saint-Pierroise (Réunion - France) - Club Brugge (Belgium) - AC Milan (Italy) - Bayern Munich (Germany)

Goals scored and number of games: 333 goals in 596 games

Goals scored internationally: 30 goals in 54 Caps.

Club trophies:

- UEFA Champions League: 1993–94 (AC Milan)
- Europa League: 1995–96 (Bayern Munich)
- Italian League: Twice 1992–93, 1993–94
- French League: 4 times 1988–89, 1989–90, 1990–91, 1991–92 (Marseille)
- French Cup: 1988–89 (Marseille)
- Belgian Cup: 1986
- Italian Super Cup: 1992, 1993

National team trophies:

- FIFA World Cup: Bronze Medalist 1986

Personal trophies:

- Ballon d'Or: 1991
- Onze d'Or: 1991
- UEFA Champions League top goal scorer: 3 times 1989–90, 1990–91, 1991–92
- FIFA World Player of the Year: Second place 1991
- Marseille's player of the 20th century

- League 1 top goal scorer: 5 times 1987–88, 1988–89, 1989–90, 1990–91, 1991–92

Career Overview

Jean –Pierre Papin is Olympic Marseille's player of the 20th Century, and one of the few who won both the Onze d'OR and the Ballon d'OR in the same year.

Papin started his career in INF Vichy; a training center established by the French federation for exploring the best of young talents in soccer. From Vichy, he grabbed Valenciennes's attention and spent one year with the club in Division 2 scoring 16 goals in 35 games, but his desire to compete at the highest levels got Papin to move to Belgium and join Club Brugge in 1985.

In Belgium, it took Papin one year to make his mark in Brugge's history, scoring 32 goals in 43 games, and helping the team win the Belgian Cup. Such outstanding performance got the club's supporters to choose Papin as the best foreign player in the history of their club established in 1891, despite the short time he sent with the club.

Papin then moved the following year, 1986, to Olympic Marseille to be part of the club's best team of all times, alongside Chris Waddle and Abedi Pele, scoring 16 goals in his debut year with the club, before winning the French golden boot in the following year after scoring 23 goals in 46 games including 19 league tables.

Prime time: 1988-1992

After coming 6th in the 1987-88 season; Marseille made Gerard Gili the head manager of the team.

In his first year with the team; Gili won the French double (League 1 and Coupe de France) after defeating Monaco in the cup final in a game that witnessed Papin scoring 3 of the 33 goals that he scored with Marseille during that season.

The next year he helped the team win their second league title in a row, after scoring 38 goals which made him the league's top scorer for the second time.

Such performance backed Papin's nomination in 1991; Papin for the best player Europe, and the world after helping Marseille win a third league title, as well as reaching the final game of the European Cup, before it was named The Champions League.

However, they lost lost on penalties against Red Star Belgrade. Papin was the tournament's top scorer with 6 goals including his famous semi-final goal against Spartak Moscow.

AC Milan

After winning his 4th league title with Marsellie and his 4th consecutive Golden Boot award, Papin left his beloved team to join AC Milan for 2 unsuccessful years for the Frenchman who, despite winning 5 titles - including 2 league medals and the 92-93 Champions league – spent most of his time on the bench.

His 31 goals however, got him a move to Munich to start a new part of his career with FC Bayern, yet again, it wasn't as successful as his period in France.

After a set of serious injuries and 6 goals -including an all-time stunner that is still being honored until now – Papin decided to leave to Bordeaux despite winning the UEFA Cup, to spend his last 3 years in France before retiring in 1999 with Guingamp.

Performance

Papin was well known for his ability to strike the ball at any time at any height and from any position with his both feet.

King of Papinades

Like Van Basten and Dennis Bergkamp, Papin was among the players who applied themselves with gusto and creativity. Watching some of his goals, Papin cared for the quality of the shots he made, the same way he cared for putting the ball inside the goal.

At any given day, Papin would prefer a first-timer or a bicycle kick on a headers or simple shots. Some of his goals are among the top 1000 goals scored since the beginning of soccer including his wonderful bicycle kick against KFC Uerdingen 05 is still among the best 50 goals scored in the German league.

From 14 yards, Papin received a cross inside the penalty area, and rather than just tap the ball on his chest, turn and send a normal shot, he twisted his body, struck the ball with all the power he had and scored a goal you could only see once in a blue moon.

Papin tendency to grab any chance to score a goal that pulls out wows and admirations was seen anywhere he played.

That tendency made the French fans call the type of volleys and acrobatic goals he scored Papinades, because no one like him had the skills and the courage to create such magic time and time again.

With Marseille, he had his famous stunner against Union Luxembourg, with Milan, his wonderful backward kick against Bologna is still remembered and with France, he had his famous goal, and again, from a bicycle kick against Denmark in Euro 1992, and it was much harder than the one he later scored for FC Bayern.

Powerful Finishing

Ever played FIFA with someone who enjoy shooting from distances than approaching the goal and scoring from inside the area? Papin was this type of players, but in the real word.

Papin enjoyed putting power behind his shots. He would always pick a position where he can benefit from the space around him to create the required power to make the shot hit wonders. Inside the area, outside the area, it didn't matter as long as he enjoyed shooting.

Jurgen Klinsmann - The Golden Bomber

Full Name: Jürgen Klinsmann
Date of birth: 30 July 1964
Nationality: German (Former West German)
Status: Retired (2003) – Currently; head coach for the American National team.

Clubs: Stuttgarter Kickers, VfB Stuttgart, Bayern Munich (Germany) - Inter Milan, Sampdoria (Italy) - AS Monaco (France) - Tottenham Hotspur (England) - Orange County Blue Star (USA)

Goals scored and number of games: 324 goals in 722 games

Goals scored internationally: 47 goals in 108 Caps

Club trophies:
- UEFA Europa League: Twice 1990–91 (Inter Milan) - 1995–96 (Bayern Munich)
- German League1996–97 (Bayern Munich)
- Italian Super Cup: 1989 (Inter Milan)

National team trophies:
- FIFA World Cup: 1990
- Euro 1996: Winner
- Euro 1992: Silver Medalist

Personal trophies:
- Ballon d'Or: Second place 1995
- Bundesliga top goal scorer: 1987–88
- German soccerer of the year: Twice 1988 (West Germany) – 1994
- Tottenham Hotspur player of the year: 1994

Career Overview

In September 1981, Jurgen Klinsmann made his debut in professional soccer playing for a team called Stuttgarter Kickers in the German second division.

It all came after his family was relocated at Stuttgart and young Klinsmann had to find himself another team beyond his original one Geislingen.

As a new player, Klinsmann spent his first few years with Kickers playing for the youth team before making it to the first team however, his debut was somehow shy, and he failed to make a noticeable impact during his first two seasons as a pro, scoring only 4 goals in 28 appearances.

The following year though, it seemed like Klinsmann's preparation period has reached its end and flourishing time was so close as he scored 21 goals in 37 games.

With this, he helped the Stuttgart-based team finish third in Bundesliga 2 and luring their rivals, and the Bundesliga champion, VfB Stuttgart to approach him with a deal, promising him a place in the team that has just won its third league title..

5 Years in Stuttgart

With Stuttgart, Klinsmann started his by scoring 17 goals in 38 games but his goals weren't enough to help the team defend its league title after coming 10th with 33 points.

However, his 3 cup goals got Stuttgart a ticket to the cup final against Bayern Munich but they lost the title to the Bavarian side after a 5-2 loss in which he scored his 4th goal in the tournament and his 20th in the entire season.

The following year he helped the team eliminate Real Madrid and reach the UEFA Cup final but they failed to raise the cup after losing the 2-legged final against Maradona and his teammates in Napoli.

Unfortunately to him, this was the maximum he could reach with Stuttgart so he decided to move somewhere else and say goodbye to the fans after scoring 57 goals during his last 3 years with the team.

In 1989, only one year before the world cup, Klinsmann made a move to the league champion Inter Milan to join the Italian's team campaign to win their first European trophy since 1965.

Swimming it to The World Cup

After scoring 15 games in his first season with Inter and helping the team win the Italian Super cup and ending third on the league table; Klinsmann was chosen by Germany's manager at that time; Franz Beckenbauer to be part of the national team competing in the 1990 world cup.

During that world cup; Klinsmann was a key player in the team; scoring in their first group stage game against the strong Yugoslavian team before scoring again in a 5-1 game against UAE.

He then followed up by a third goal in the Round of 16 against Netherlands' all-star team which had players like Ronald Koeman, Frank Rijkaard, Ruud Gullit and the best player in the world; Marco Van Basten.

However; Klinsmann's best performance in the tournament was in the final game against Argentina when he lead a dangerous attack from the right wing before faking being tackled by Argentina's defender Pedro Monzon who got a direct red card 25 minutes before the end of the game.

Then 20 minutes before Klinsmann successfully and sneakily won a penalty kick in the 85th after he waited until he was approached by one of Argentina's defenders inside the penalty kick before diving inside the box, forcing the referee to call for a penalty kick that was later scored by his German teammate in Inter; Andreas Brehme.

From Inter to Tottenham

After winning the UEFA Cup final against Roma in 1991, Klinsmann spent another season with Inter but with too many problems in the team, especially after failing to qualify to the European championships he decided to leave to AS Monaco with which he scored 20 league goals and helped the team reach the semifinals of the European cup.

The following year he joined Tottenham Hotspurs in the English league after feeling that the people in the French club lacked the ambition to win something big.

In London however, he didn't receive the welcoming he desired as both the English fans and media couldn't forget his attempts to fake a penalty against England in the semifinals of the world cup.

However, this all changed, at least for Spurs' fans, with the 30 magnificent goals he scored during his first spell with Tottenham which got him to win the German best player award and the PFA award for the best player in the English league.

In fact; Klinsmann's impact on Tottenham is still felt until now despite spending only one year with the team. Every Tottenham still remembers how his 21 league goals helped the team finish – for the last time- above Arsenal; their biggest rival.

Performance

Klinsmann had it all, speed, dribbling and powerful finishing and no defense in the world could stop him on a day when everything went his way.

The Cassic Fox in The Box

Klinsmann was the classic sniper inside the penalty area waiting for anything to catch.

Despite some glimpses of mastery –like his acrobatic backward kick against FC Bayern – Klinsmann preferred simplicity over style. He was a very reliable player who knows where to stand and how to finish, with an excellent anticipation for lost balls.

Prepare and Score

No doubt, Klinsmann is among the 10 best players I've ever seen in what I call, using foot on demand. Not only he could score with both feet, he had the skill of quickly shifting balance of his body generate enough power to shoot the ball using the nearest foot not the dominant one.

I recall two incidents for him, the first was his famous goal against South Korea in the 1994 World Cup when he slightly chipped the ball with his right to turn 180 degrees and hit it with his left.

The second was in a league game against Roma when he marched the ball with the right foot and when chased by 2 defenders while running and realizing he can't use his right foot to shoot the ball, he marvelously switched the balance of his body to his left foot and struck the ball from almost 30 yards towards Roma's net.

The Trouble Maker

Klinsmann was willing to do anything to get a penalty, including diving, and faking injuries. Ant though, this may sound unethical – and it is indeed – it was a sign to how bad he liked to win.

Besides, this also gave him immunity against defenders and the space he needed to score goals, since they all knew he would grab any chance to win a foul or get them sent off like he did in the 1990 World Cup.

He did it with almost every team he played for yet he never felt bad about it, in fact when he later moved to England in 1994, Klinsmann celebrated his 30 goals with Tottenham with a dive as a sign of not caring about what the English media said about him and his "unethical" ways of winning.

Bebeto - The Crybaby

Full Name: José Roberto Gama de Oliveira
Date of birth: February 16, 1964
Nationality: Brazilian
Status: Retired (2002)
Clubs: Vitória, Flamengo, Vasco da Gama, Cruzeiro, Botafogo (Brazil) - Deportivo La Coruña, Sevilla (Spain) - Toros Neza (Mexico) - Kashima Antlers (Japan) - Al-Ittihad (KSA)
Goals scored and number of games: 217 goals in 416 games
Goals scored internationally: 39 goals in 75 Caps
Club trophies:
- Brazilian League: Twice 1983 (Flamengo) & 1989 (Vasco da Gama)
- Spanish Cup (Copa del Rey): 1995 (Deportivo La Coruña)
- Spanish Super Cup: 1995 (Deportivo La Coruña)

National team trophies:
- FIFA World Cup: Winner 1994
- FIFA U-20 World Cup: Winner 1983
- FIFA Confederations Cup: 1997
- Copa América: 1989
- Olympic games: Silver Medalist (1992) & Bronze Medalist (1996)

Personal trophies:
- Best player in Brazil: 1992
- South American Soccerer of the Year: 1989
- Copa América top scorer: 1989
- Spanish League top scorer (El Pichichi: 1989
- List of the 100 greatest soccerers of all time by World Soccer magazine

Career Overview

Bebeto started his career in soccer playing for Vitoria Sporting Club before impressing Flamengo's executives who signed the 19 year old wonder kid in 1983 after helping the Brazilian team win the U-20 World Cup which they won after defeating Argentina 1-0 in the final game.

Knowing for his playmaking skills; young Bebeto scored 34 goals in 80 games, forming a magnificent companionship with Zico, his childhood hero.

The highlight of his period at Flamengo however, was the double he scored in the league finalgame against Internacional which secured the 4th league title for Flamengo.

For his skills at both goal scoring, and playmaking, Bebeto received an invitation to be part of the Brazilian Olympic team competing the same year, 1988, in Seoul, South Korea.

He helped Brazil reach the gold-medal game after eliminating West Germany from the semifinals. However, a loss in the extra time against the Soviet Union made them win silver.

Things seemed like going well with Bebeto however, upon arriving from South Korea, he announced an unexpected move and left Flamengo to join the archrival, Vasco da Gama to help them win the league after scoring 6 goals in the last 6 games of the season 7 weeks before winning both the gold medal and the golden boot award in the 1989 Copa America.

Such performance later got him to win the "South American soccer of the year" award for his success on both the domestic, and the international sides.

Two Unsuccessful Years and a Move to Spain

The following two years weren't so good for Bebeto who suffered from injury and scored only 4 goals in 16 games with Vasco De Gama.

However, things dramatically changed for him when he scored 18 goals in 25 appearances on his third year with Vasco despite not winning any major trophy that year. So, he decided to leave and make a move to Spain and join Deportivo La Coruna.

Bebto's move literally transformed l Dépor" and changed it from being the mid-table team that frequently fights for avoiding relegation to a strong contender and a team that fought both Real Madrid and Barcelona on the league title.

In 3 years, La Coruna dramatically and strangely lost 3 league titles the first was in 1992-93 in which the team came third, only 4 points behind Barcelona.

The second was in 1993-94 when Deportivo lost the league title to Barcelona on goal differences and the third was in 1994-95 when they came second behind Real Madrid despite winning 6 of their last 7 league games.

In his 4 years in Spain; Bebeto scored 86 goals in 131 games including a goal against Real Madrid in the Spanish Super cup which Deportivo won in 1995 after winning the Spanish cup in the same year.

Bebeto also managed – during the same period – to help Brazil win its 4th world cup title in 1994 after scoring 3 times including two important goals in the Round-of-16 game against USA (1-0) and the quarter-final game against Netherlands (3-2).

His Ro-Ro duet with Romario was what helped Brazil win the cup after participating in 9 of the 11 goals that Brazil has scored in the tournament.

What was also noticeable with Bebeto in the world cup was his famous dance against Netherlands which was played 72 hours after his third son was born.

Back to Brazil and Retirement

After failing to win the league title for the fourth time; Bebeto decided to leave Deportivo La Coruna and move to Brazil.

In summer 1996 he signed with his old team; Flamengo scoring 7 times in his first 15 appearances with the team however he left in the same season to join the Spanish team; Sevilla with which he only played 5 games before moving back to Brazil to spend one year with Vitoria.

After this, he keaved again and spending his next 8 years with 6 different teams before retiring in Al-Ittihad in the Saudi Arabian league.

Bebeto and Romario: The Golden Duo

Not too many people know the two players who formed the most famous soccer-duo in the past 30 years were enemies and couldn't even stand sitting next to each other in the same dressing room for almost 8 years before the 1994 world cup.

Known for his outgoing, slightly aggressive, macho-type behavior, Romario wasn't a big fan of Bebeto's attitude both on and off the field. Romario didn't like his teammate's shyness or the way he kept asking referees for fouls anytime he got hit on the field.

Bebeto was also his rival, competing against him when they both played in Brazil and even when he left Netherlands to join Barcelona, Bebeto was there to compete with Romario for the 1994 league title – which went to Barcelona on goal difference – and the goal scoring title as well.

All that made Romario publicly declare he can't stand Bebeto and didn't like the idea of both being on the same side, but all that changed in summer 1994, when both players had to put their conflicts aside and focus on helping the Brazilian team win its first World Cup title in 20 years.

With his talent at creating streams of chances, Bebeto helped the world class finisher, Romario, score 5 goals in the tournament and the both participated in 10 of the 11 goals scored by Brazil in that tournament to end the world cup with 2 gold medals and a friendship that is still alive until today.

Performance

Too bad a player with such qualities didn't leave to Europe at a very young age, Bebeto would've made an excellent impact in if he went there earlier than moving to Spain at the age of 28.

He was magnificently amazing compared to how small he was.

Super-FAST

Bebeto had one theme repeated in most of his goals, a long ball then he comes from behind, outruns a defender and scores. He was very fast and this allowed him to average a goal every two games throughout his entire career despite not playing for any of Europe's most competitive clubs.

Another quality Bebeto had added to the list of his skills was his ability to play with both feed equally, and without any problem. At his best, Bebeto was a master dribbler, able to go past the strongest of defenders without blinking. He would move the ball around his body, swerve, and run smoothly without getting caught.

The speed he got was there in the moment he stole the ball from the Dutch defense, made a wonderful dribble past the keeper and scored Brazil's second in the World Cup quarter final.

It was his key to score his famous run against Real Madrid when he came right from behind Madrid's defense at great speed and stole the ball right before the goalkeeper to score in the empty net.

Excellent in Headers

At 1.78m, it didn't seem possible to score that amount of headers in one career, yet Bebeto was different. He compensated his size with his smart positioning and technique that enabled him to beat many of the world's strongest, and tallest defenders throughout his career.

One of which was against Denmark in France 1998, when he positioned himself between the Danish defense to score a header against the world's best goalkeeper at that time, Peter Schmeichel.

A Free-Kick Genius

Bebeto had a very strong foot that allowed him to practice shooting whenever the chance was available, and also helped him score lots of goals from free kicks.

His technique was simple; stay close to the ball, and twist your body while raising the ball above the wall. It didn't require lots of power, but enough practice to make scoring a foul looks easier than it really is.

Ivan Zamorano - Ivan the Terrible

Full Name: Iván Luis Zamorano Zamora
Date of birth: January 18, 1967
Nationality: Chilean
Status: Retired (2003)
Clubs: Cobresal, Cobreandino, Colo-Colo (Chile) - St. Gallen (Switzerland) - Sevilla, Real Madrid (Spain) - Inter Milan (Italy) - Club America (Mexico)
Goals scored and number of games: 382 goals in 681 games
Goals scored internationally: 34 goals in 69 Caps
Club trophies:
- UEFA Europa League: 1997–98 (Inter Milan)
- Spanish League (La Liga): 1994–95 (Real Madrid)
- Spanish Cup (Copa del Rey): 1993(Real Madrid)
- Spanish Super Cup: 1993(Real Madrid)
- Chile Cup: 1987 (Cobresal)
- Mexican Premier Division: 2002

National team trophies:
- Olympic Bronze Medal: 2000

Personal trophies:
- La Liga Best Foreign Player: 1994-95
- Spanish League top scorer (El Pichichi): 1994–95

Career Overview

Zamorano started his career in Cobresal who loaned him to the team that competes in the Chilean second division; Trasandino de Los Andes with which he scored 27 goals in 29 games.

This was enough for Cobresal to bring him back to the team and help them sin the Chilean cup before leaving to Switzerland to join St. Gallen FC after scoring 35 games in the 29 games he played wearing Cobresal's T-shirt.

From Switzerland to Span

With St. Gallen, Zamorano spent two amazing years, scoring 35 goals in 55 games which caught the attention of the scout managers of the Spanish club; Sevilla who made him cut his third season with St. Gallen to make to move to Spain in 1991-92 season.

And in his first season with the team; Zamorano (23 years old at the time) scored 10 goals in 31 games before scoring another 13 the next year which made Real Madrid approach Sevilla with a 5 million dollar deal.

This was enough to convince the young Chilean to join Real Madrid and help them win the league title after losing it to Barcelona twice in the previous 2 years.

Success in Madrid

In his first year with Real Madrid; Zamorano scored 37 goals in 45 games helping the team win the Spanish cup against Real Zaragoza before they dramatically lose the league title after finishing second and only one point behind Barcelona; the league winner.

However; Zamorano took his revenge after scoring twice against Barcelona in December 1993, helping Real Madrid win its 4th super cup title.

Real Madrid finally won the league in May 1995 and the club owed it to Zamorano who scored a remarkable 28 goals which not only helped Madrid win its 26th league title (9 points above Barcelona) but also made Zamorano Spain's top goal scorer and the winner of the golden boot or "El Pichichi".

Inter Milan

In his quest to win the club's first league title since 1989; Inter Milan's new president; Massimo Moratti brought Ronaldo from Barcelona and Zamorano from Real Madrid to help the team that came seventh on the 1995-96 league table.

In his first year with the team; Zamorano wore a t-shirt with (8+1) on it since t-shirt number 9 was taken by Ronaldo who left 10 to the newcomer; Roberto Baggio. And in his first season, he helped Inter win the 1998 UEFA Cup Final after scoring in a 3-0 win against Lazzio in the "Parc des Princes" stadium in Paris.

He then spent 4 more seasons with the team; scoring 40 goals in 148 games before he joined Club América with which he won the Mexican league in 2001-02 after scoring 18 goals in 35 league games.

The Golden duo: Salas and Zamorano

One of the best duos in the history of Latin soccer was formed between Ivan Zamorano and his Chilean teammate and best friend Marcelo Salas between 1994 and 2001.

They helped create a strong reputation for the Chilean national team by their outstanding performance in 1998 when they helped Chile qualify to the competition for the first time since 1982 before they assist and score 4 of the 5 goals scored by Chile in the tournament.

They also helped the Chilean team reach the semifinal game of the 1999 Copa America before they lose against Uruguay on penalties. Combined and in 70 appearances; Zamorano and Salas scored 71 goals for Chile.

Performance

Zamorano was like a Cobra inside the penalty box. He seemed harmful but from nowhere he could strike with the speed of light and score!

Power, aggression, and warrior-like attitude

Zamorano wasn't the kind of player who can be scared easily, I guess playing for Atletico Madrid would be a perfect fit for him if he decides to come back from his retirement again.

He was quite similar to Atletico's coach, Diego Simeone, with the same bravery and the same warrior-like attitude.

Similar to Marceloa Salas, both had a touch of aggressiveness and power on everything they do on the field.

For instance, Zamorano's was nicknamed Ivan the Terrible after the powerful Russian prince who was known for using extreme power and violence with his opponents.

He was also nicknamed El Bam Bam for the extreme power he shows when hitting the ball with either head or foot.

Excellent Jumping Technique

Zamorano was brilliant at air plays. He was excellent in winning challenges over defenders, regardless of their size.

Despite playing in the physically demanding La Liga and the Serie A, he could easily win any ball in the air and direct it to wherever he wanted in and outside the penalty area.

The key to his success was his courage and not being afraid to collapse in the air with defenders as well as his jumping technique that made him overcome not being tall enough to play inside the box. I recall his 12-yards header against Cagliari while playing for Inter Milan.

I was watching that game live – I'm a huge Inter fan – and during the first 15 minutes of the game he played two headers, both at least 10 yards away from the goal, the first was saved by the keeper, while the second was extremely brilliant.

He received a long pass not from the side, but from center - which makes it even harder – and from a difficult position, with two defenders around him, he struck a long header that hit the left side of Cagliari's net.

A Very Strong Right Foot

Like I told you earlier, Zamorano was excellent at anything related to power, especially when it came down to shooting.

He, like Puscas, preferred to strike with power rather than place the ball with style. He could do it with his left foot as well as his right one. The best example on this was the first of the three goals he scored against Barcelona in Madrid's 5-0 win in El Classico.

He received a pace from a difficult angle, and rather than send a cross or try to be stylish, he struck the ball with all the power he had knowing that no keeper would dare saving it even from a dead angle.

A Team Player

When he left Real Madrid to join Inter, he was known for his finishing skills and his role as a typical, number-9 however, after the coming of Ronaldo in 1997, he found himself forced to either accept playing less frequently or adapt to a new role in the team, and he successfully and smartly did it.

Since that year, Zamorano developed himself and used all the technical and tactical skills he had to become a team player who would help other teammates, like Alvaro Recoba, create more chances rather than score them himself.

Stats show his goal-scoring rates dropped dramatically since he joined Inter, yet what stats failed to show was the number of assists and chances he created per game.

Between 1996 and 1999, Zamorano was among Europe's top playmakers with at least 12 assists per season despite being a plain center forward, and such development in his performance is a clear sign for how talented this player was.

Rivaldo - The Extraordinary

Full Name: Rivaldo Vítor Borba Ferreira

Date of birth: 19 April 1972

Nationality: Brazilian

Status: Retired (2015)

Clubs: Santa Cruz, Mogi Mirim, Corinthians,São Paulo,São Caetano, Palmeiras (Brazil) - Deportivo La Coruña, Barcelona (Spain) - AC Milan (Italy) - Olympiacos, AEK Athens (Greece) - Bunyodkor (Uzbekistan) - Kabuscorp (Angola)

Goals scored and number of games: 326 goals in 710 games

Goals scored internationally: 35 goals in 74 Caps

Club trophies:
-   UEFA Champions League: 2002-2003 (AC Milan)
-   UEFA Super Cup: Twice 1997 (Barcelona), 2003 (AC Milan)
-   Spanish League: Twice 1997-1998, 1998-1999
-   Spanish Cup: 1997-1998
-    Italian Cup: 2002-2003
-   Brazilian League: 1994 (Palmeiras)
-   Greek Super League: 3 times 2005, 2006, 2007 (Olympiacos)
-   Greek Cup: Twice 2005, 2006 (Olympiacos)

National team trophies:
-   FIFA World Cup: Winner 2002
-   FIFA World Cup: Silver Medalist 1998
-   Confederations Cup: 1997
-   Copa America: 1999
-   Olympic games: Bronze Medalist 1996

Personal trophies:
-   Ballon d'Or: 1999

- Onze d'Or: 1999
- World Soccer Player of the Year: 1999
- Best forward in Brazil: Twice 1993. 1994
- Copa America top scorer: 1999
- Greek Championship best foreign player: Twice 2006, 2007

Career Overview

Rivaldo was born in Paulista in Brazil in 1972. His family was so poor that he lost the majority of his front teeth at the age of five because of malnutrition. Such poverty forced him to work every morning before spending his nights playing soccer with his young friends.

However, despite the passion he had for soccer – which he carried away throughout his career – young Rivaldo was rejected from several youth teams as coaches and scouts admitted that he was physically weak to become a prolific soccer player.

He was rejected at the age of 14 from both Corinthians and Paulistano, yet his persistence got the later to sign him two years later in 1989 before moving the following year to Santa Cruz to begin his pro career, scoring 6 league goals in 14 appearances.

He then joined Mogi Mirim and scored 10 goals in the second division before becoming the talk of the entire country after scoring a magnificent goal for Mirim in the second division after sending a lob-shot above the opponent's keeper only 5 seconds from the beginning of the game.

That goal got Corinthians to watch him carefully before signing him in a loan deal for a year in which Rivaldo scored 11 times in 30 games but rather than stay at Corinthians, he accepted an offer from the league champion at that time, Palmeiras, and joined their club in summer 1994.

From Palmeiras to Spain

In Palmerias; Rivaldo helped the team win a second league title and two Paulista leagues (the regional league of Sao Paulo).

He then helped the team reach the cup final game in 1996 but they lost to Cruzeiro and in May 1996, the Spanish club, Deportivo La Coruna, announced the signing of the Brazilian midfielder for a $6 million deal.

That year, Rivaldo proved his value to the fans of Blues and Whites, and scored 21 goals in all competition including 16 league goals that helped Deportivo finish third behind Real Madrid and Barcelona.

Such performance grabbed the attention of Barcelona's coach; Sir Bobby Robson insisted that the club should sign the Brazilian at any cost, and this is exactly what happened in summer 1997 when Barcelona purchased Rivaldo from Deprotivo La Coruna for $26 million.

A few months before scoring and assisting in a 3-1 win against the European champion of the year, Borussia Dortmund, in the European Super cup.

In that year; Rivaldo helped Barcelona win the Spanish double and was chosen as the best player of the year before adding more wood to the fire and winning his second league title in a row in 1999, the same year he was picked as the best player in both Europe and the World, ahead of Manchester United's David Beackham.

Louis van Gaal: Rise and Fall

If there's one problem with the Dutch coach; Louis van Gaal then it will be stubbornness.

Van Gaal , who was appointed after his massive success with Ajax Amsterdam, didn't like the fact that the Catalan team depended completely on Rivaldo. So did he do?

He played him on the left wing, without giving him the freedom to play as he liked and do his magic.

Even though this move proved to be ineffective, Van Gaal insisted on it and wasted on Barcelona an excellent chance to win the league title that was later won by Deportivo La Coruna in the year 2000. That year, and for the first time since he wore Barcelona's jersey, Rivaldo failed to become one of the league's top 10 goal scorers..

The next year wasn't good for Barcelona after Van Gaal was scaked from his position, but unlike his coach; Rivaldo had a better season and was so close from becoming the league's top goalscorer with the 23 goals he scored in 2001.

This included a wonderful bicycle kick against Valencia in the 90th minute which helped Barça secure the league's 4th position and qualify to the Champions league competitions the following year which was his last year with Barcelona.

During this year he spent most of the following season on the bench of Van Gaal who was again hired to manage the team in 2002 after spending one and a half year with the Dutch national team.

The 4R and The World Cup

In June 2002; the Brazilian team amazed the entire world with their world class performance in the world cup that was held in both Japan and South Korea.

Together; Ronaldo, Rivaldo, Ronaldinho and Roberto Carlos scored 17 goals including 8 goals for Ronaldo (the golden boot winner) and 6 for Rivaldo who showed the world how Van Gaal was wrong for kicking him out of Barcelona.

Such performance made him sign a 3 deal contract with AC Milan in summer 2002 to help the team defeat the enemy, Juventus, on penalty kicks in the final game that was played in the famous Old Trafford stadium.

He then helped Milan defeat Porto in the European Super Cup before raising the Italian cup with the team after defeating Roma 6-3 in a two-legged final.

From Milan to Greece

After spending most of his second year with Milan benched, Rivaldo moved back to Brazil for one season before joining Greece's biggest club, Olympiacos with which he won 3 consecutive league titles as well as 2 Greek cups in between 2005 and 2007.

He scored 41 goals in 84 games with the team before spending his next 8 years moving between Angola, Greece again and Uzbekistan including a successful year with Sao Caetano with which he scored 29 goals at the age of 40 before finally retiring last year at the age of 43 in Mogi Grim; the club he previously played for and the club he now owns.

Performance

His clumsy movement on the pitch didtn look impressive at first sight, but as soon as he received the ball you realized that this was one of the best strikers ever.

Excellent Shooting Skills

As someone who likes to watch volleys and first timers, my entertainment anytime I watched Brazil would begin the moment any of these 2 decides to take a shot, Roberto Carlos or Rivaldo.

Rivaldo was the type of players shining better outside the penalty area. Give him the ball, anywhere, and he'll find a perfect shooting spot, no matter how tight the defense he faced or how good the goalkeeper was, Rivaldo will always amaze you.

I still remember his goal against Venezuela in the World Cup qualifications, he received a through pass from Ronaldo and rather than wait on the ball, he struck it with all the power he had and the ball went inside the goal and came out again. And his two goals against Thailand in the 2000 King's Cup.

The first was a 28 yard low shot while the second was a remarkable, mystifying +40, impossible that is sure to be one of the best goals in Brazil's history with soccer. And they weren't just long, strong shots that he made successfully, Rivaldo had an excellent eye when shooting from outside the 18 yard area.

One of his best, most beautiful goals was scored against Rayo Vallecano in the Spanish League. Rivaldo had the ball near the penalty area with 5 defenders against him, and rather than directly shoot the ball or pass it to Marc Overmars or Emmanuel Petit, he chipped it over the 5 defenders and their goalkeeper.

Assisting Skills

When being asked about the player he preferred playing by his side, Ronaldo didn't choose Zinedine Zidane, David Beckham or Luis Figo, instead, he chose Rivaldo, who understood him better than anyone else.

Rivaldo was smart to understand his roles in the game. With Brazil Rivaldo a different version from the one we saw in Barcelona. He still scored, but he played more for the unit rather than being the team's only superstar.

With Brazil, Rivaldo was the dynamic player not sticking to one role on the field. One time he was on top of the penalty area, the other moment he's on the left wing sending crosses to Ronaldo.

His passes were amazing, especially the ones from long distances. He would send a through pass from 30 or 40 yards, to the right man and no matter where this teammate was standing or how many defenders are around, it will always fit perfectly.

I remember his game against Turkey in the group stage of the 2002 World Cup. In that game,

Rivaldo had the ball near the left wing and Ronaldo was close to the penalty area, surrounded by 3 defenders and it seemed impossible to get the ball to Ronaldo's position, not mentioning scoring from it, but Rivaldo with a magical touch, sent a curvy assist right at Ronaldo's right foot and to score Brazil's first goal in the game.

The passion to Play

Not so many people know that Rivaldo retired from soccer only last year, and at the age of 42. Rivaldo's passion for the game got him to buy his old team, Mogi Grim, just to find a place to play in regardless of his age.

He wasn't the type of players who would surround himself with lots of models, or come out with weird statements to grab the media's attention.

Like Jairzinho and Socrates, Rivaldo was an unknown legend who fought his way through poverty just to enjoy what he liked best, playing soccer.

Eric Cantona - The King

Eric

Full Name: Eric Cantona
Date of birth: 24 May 1966
Nationality: French
Status: Retired (1997)
Clubs: Auxerre, Marseille, Bordeaux, Montpellier, Martigues, Nîmes (France) - Leeds United, Manchester United (England)
Goals scored and number of games: 185 goals in 485 games
Goals scored internationally: 20 goals in 45 Caps
Club trophies:
- English League: 5 times 1991-92 (Leeds United) , 1992–93, 1993–94, 1995–96, 1996–97 (Manchester United)
- French League: Twice 1988–89, 1990–91 (Marseille)
- English Cup: Twice 1993–94, 1995–96 (Manchester United)
- French Cup: 1989–90 (Montpellier)
- English Super Cup: 4 times 1992 (Leeds United), 1993, 1994, 1996 (Manchester United)

National team trophies:
- UEFA European Under-21 Soccer Championship: 1988

Personal trophies:
- Ballon d'Or: Third Place 1993
- Onze d'Or: 1996
- English soccerer of the year: 1995–96

Career Overview

Cantona started his youth career playing goalkeeper in Sports Olympiques Caillols, a famous amateur team established in 1939.

He first started playing as a goalkeeper however a year in this position made him realize he belonged up at the front where he could score and enjoy more time with the ball.

At the age of 15 he made a move to Auxerre in which he spent 4 on-and-off years before he made his first impact in soccer in 1987 when he scored 13 league goals to help Auxerre finish fourth, only 6 points behind the league champions, Bordeaux.

Such performance gave him the chance to join Olympic Marseille the following year, but despite doing well in the French league (which will later be won by Marseille).

His aggressiveness and lack of anger management got him into a series of problems and bans started with a fight with the fans and ended with a one-year ban from playing for the national team after calling the team's coach, Henry Michelle, a scumbag (Un sac à merde) live on TV.

Such attitude forced Marseille to loan him to Bordeaux for the rest of the season before sending him in another loan deal, the following year, to Montpellier with which he scored four times in six games and helped the club, that has just came out from the second division, to win the French cup for the first time in 61 years.

Such performance got Marseille to bring him back to help them win their third league title in a row however, problems again with the club's chairman got him to leave to league-2 champions, Nîmes Olympique.

This because he had another bizarre incident when he threw the ball at the referee in one league game which got him to receive another ban, this time for 2 months, which made him decide to retire from soccer for a while.

However, he then changed his mind 2 months later and decided, on his psychoanalyst advice, to start a new leaf in England and play for Leeds United which has been doing great since the team promoted to division one the year before.

With Leeds, Cantona participated in 9 goals in the remaining 15 games of the season to help the club win their first league title in 18 years yet the following year, he moved to Man United for $4 million to add the final piece of puzzle to Alex Ferguson squad that later dominated the English soccer for years.

Making History

In Manchester, Ferguson knew he had to slightly lessen his grip on Cantona so he can bring his best. He allowed him to come late and wear whatever he wanted to trainings as he knew Cantona was the key to turning United to a non-stop trophy-winning machine and it did happen.

As in 5 years, Cantona blasted and flourished, participating in 127 goals with the club and helping them win 10 titles including the English Double (the league and the FA cup) twice in 94 and 96 yet again.

His aggression and lack of self-discipline got him through multiple problems in England including his crazy moment against Crystal Palace when kicked Palace's defender and got sent off before throwing a kung-fu kick at one of Palace's fans. He was charged with assault, imprisoned for 2 weeks and banned from playing soccer for 8 months.

The following year however, he made a magnificent after-ban debut with Manchester, scoring once and assisting once in a win against the enemy, Liverpool, in Old Trafford. He then repeated it again, and scored a late winner against Liverpool in the FA Cup final. He raised the cup as Manchester's new captain and helped the team win the double in 1996.

Early Retirement

After helping United win their second league title in a row, it was apparent for Cantona he won't be part of Aimé Jacquet's squad competing in the 1998 World Cup. Cantona realized he won't be able to fulfill his dream since the French coach didn't want problems in his team's dressing room.

He saw Zinedine Zindane a better substitute for him, so he decided to retire completely from soccer and in May 1997, he announced that he would retire to try his luck as an actor.

Performance

If he woke up on the right side he could score on any defense in the world, but if he did the opposite he could easily lose his temper and cause another scandal.

Confidence, Charisma and Style

Everything about Cantona spoke about style or probably a deep sense of self love. From the way he raised the collar of his t-shirt to the way he liked to score his goals. This confidence and charisma was very essential for a team who hasn't won any major trophies in years.

Back, before 1992, England had only four clubs can be called trophy winners, Liverpool, Everton, Arsenal and Aston Villa…Manchester United was totally out of the trophy game, and in soccer, when a club puts an identity on, it's hard to get it back off again.

Simply, the name "Manchester United" made no other team afraid before Alex Ferguson and Eric Cantona. The club was doing well, winning the League Cup and the UEFA Cup Winners' Cup

Yet, the identity and character Manchester had in the late 90s and throughout the new millennium stemmed from the confidence Cantona gave to his teammates when he joined the team in January 1992.

Before he came, untied weren't the champions of England with only 7 league titles, the last of which was in 1967. He took his winning mentality and character and mixed them with Alex Ferguson's tactical genius to bring trophies to Old Trafford

It's fair to say the dominance and the winning attitude Manchester United has been having in the past twenty-some years was first ignited by these two. He took the team to a new level and brought something special to them.

About this, Philippe Auclair, the author of "Cantona: The rebel who would be king" says:

"The goal scoring stats for Man United before and after Cantona are so drastically contrasting. He's the reason who made Manchester United a league-winning machine."

His courage and confidence that made him dare to dribble past defenders and score solo goals steadily was the key to him being one of the best players to ever win the sacred number 7 t-shirt in Manchester.

In 5 years after he joined United, he was already winning 4 league titles, 2 FA Cups and 3 Community Shield titles (the English Super cup).

That goal he scored, and the way he pumped his chest in Old Trafford when he celebrated his goal against Tottenham sums it all when talking about Cantona's skills and style.

He dribbled past 3 defenders, made a 1-2 pass with Brian McClair, chipped the ball over the keeper's head, then celebrated like a boss without even smiling.

Was he arrogant? Maybe, but that doesn't matter in soccer, and what matters is what fans want to see. They pay for tickets and the want to see players hitting nets and winning games. And Cantona was their favorite type of players.

An Excellent Sense of Timing

Cantona wasn't the quickest on the field – in fact he sometimes seemed a little bit overweight – yet he had an excellent sense of timing that allowed him to score a lot without moving much. He was the type of players who would create danger without having the ball.

He would sneak behind defenders, switch his position frequently, and stay as close as possible to the opposite goal. This was the key to scoring some of his important goals for United, by laying low, taking the right position and waiting for the opportunity to come.

Alex Ferguson once said: *"You can teach an attacker how to struck a ball, but you can't teach him how to position himself. This should come naturally. "*

Penalty Kicks Master

From 82 goals for United, 18 of them were from the penalty spot. That means 22% of his goals which is enough to show how good Cantona was at taking penalties. His technique was simple, yet effective. He just picked a side and hit the ball, nothing fancy about it, yet he always scored.

Gabriel Batistuta – Batigol

Full Name: Gabriel Omar Batistuta

Date of birth: 1 February 1969 (age

Nationality: Argentinian

Status: Retired (2005)

Clubs: Newell's Old Boys, River Plate, Boca Juniors (Argentina) - Fiorentina, Roma, Inter Milan (Italy) - Al Arabi (Qatar)

Goals scored and number of games: 354 goals in 608 games

Goals scored internationally: 56 goals in 78 Caps

Club trophies:

- Italian League (Serie A): 2000–01 (Roma)
- The Argentinian Primer División: 1989–90 (River Plate)
- Italian Cup: 1995–96 (Fiorentina)
- Italian Super Cup: Twice 1996 (Fiorentina) and 2001 (Roma)

National team trophies:

- Copa América: 1991, 1993
- FIFA Confederations Cup: 1992

Personal trophies:

- Argentina's top Scorer of all times
- Fiorentina's top scorer of all times
- Italy's Top Scorer: 1994–95
- FIFA World Cup Silver Shoe: 1998
- Copa América's Top Scorer: 1991, 1995
- FIFA World Player of the Year: Third Place
- FIFA's list of the greatest 100 soccerers of all times

Career Overview

Batistuta started his career in soccer playing for leisure in a local club in Reconquista, Argentina and unlike many other players, it took scouts a lot of time and effort to convince him to consider joining one of their youth academies.

This because as young Batistuta was more concerned about his academic future than his soccer career that he conditioned on Newell's Old Boys scouts to find him a place in their dorms to live and study so he can later get a degree.

This all started when a game was scheduled between the national youth team and one of the regional clubs in Santa Fe however, the game was postponed and out of frustration, the coach of the national team chose to play the same day against one of the local clubs around….The one Batistuta played for.

That day, Batistuta's team won the game with 2 goals to 1, and he was the one to score both goals, and by the end of the game he was approached by many scouts luring him to join one of their systems yet, he wasn't sure about what to do with his life and he refused to say yes.

However, seeing how well he played, one of these scouts brought a friend of his who worked at the league champion, Newell's Old Boys, and went directly to Batistuta's father to convince his kid to join Newell's which eventually, and finally, happened by the end of 1986.

With Newell's, Batistuta – a huge Boca Juniors fan -
made his debut at the age of 20, in 1988, and scored 7
goals in 21 games which brought him an offer from
the Argentine giants, River Plate.

But, despite the rivalry between Boca and Plate, he
chose to sign for them in summer 1989 only to spend
the majority of the year benched by the coach Daniel
Passarella who only gave him 19 games to play -
mostly as a substitute – in which he only scored three
times.

Such neglect got 21 year old Batitstuta to accept the
offer he has been waiting for from Boca Juniors and in
that year 1991, he made his best performances and
helped Boca win the Clausura with 11 goals (the top
scorer) before scoring a winner against Colombia in
the final game of the 1991 Copa America.

This early winner against Colombia was his sixth
goal in the tournament and got him to win the golden
boot trophy.

The Tale of Fiorentina

In 1991, Fiorentina sent some of his scouts to
watch a young Argentine player called Diego Latorre,
an attacking midfielder and a friend of Batitstuta.

However, when they watched the later and his six
goals in Copa America, they decided Batistuta should
be the target of their club and in summer 1991 he was
officially a player for the Viola to score 13 impressive
goals in his first season and help the team avoid
relegation.

However, the following year and despite his 19 goals, the team was relegated and Batistuta was free to join Real Madrid, Milan, Manchester United, or any of the big clubs going after him yet he chose to stay with the team and help the club move back to Serie A which happened the following year thanks to his 16 Serie-B goals.

He then helped Firoentina win their first title in 21 years after scoring 8 goals in 8 games to get the team their fifth Italian Cup title in the history of the club before adding another title to their trophy cabinet after scoring twice against Atalanta in the 1996 super cup.

The One Missing Title

In 1999, and after being chosen as the best foreign player in Italy, Batitstuta realized that Fiorentina wouldn't be able to win the league in the near future and with one or two years left for him to play with top form, he decided to move to Roma and play under Fabio Capello in his seek to win the club first league title since 1983.

So, the most expensive deal for a 30 year old player was made in summer 2000, and Batistuta made one of his best performances in his life as he netted 20 times in 28 league games and ended the year with a league medal in his trophy room.

Performance

Batigol could score from anything at any time, a real striker who didn't feared any opponent at the soccer field.

Powerful Shots

The fact he was called "The Animal" might put you into perspective about how strong and powerful Batistuta was. When interviewed, the man who spotted him while playing in Santa Fe, said:

"When I first watched him – Batitsuta – I told myself I must get that Big kid. He can strike the ball with power and send it anywhere he wanted."

Everything about Batistuta spoke power. Tackles, headers, free kicks, penalties and long shots, all had power written all over them.

He wasn't the type of player who would just bend the ball and watch it slowly enters the ball, he loved to shoot whenever he had the chance, and the freedom he had, especially at Fiorentina, allowed him to practice this hobby at a wide range.

His both feet were so strong that, according to Maradona, he could play with a rugby ball and still score at ease.

Two of this Macho-type of goals were scored against England's strongest team in the late 90s, Manchester United and Arsenal.

The first was in Old Trafford, a world class long shot from 30 yards after a slip through the second most expensive defender in the world, Jaap Stam.

A few months before, Batigoal threw himself the ball past Marc Overmars before sending a strong ball from a tiny angle that thunderstruck David Seaman and his teammates.

Powerful Free Kicks

With more than 30 goals in his career – not mentioning the ones that hit the bar - , Batistuta has goals scored from free kicks more than any other center forward in his time.

He used to play his fouls the same way he struck his long shots, move away from the ball, and hit it as hard as you can, then do your famous machine-gun celebration.

Seriously, Batistuta was one of the few who made scoring a free kick from 35 or even 40 yards look easy. His free kicks were pure demonstration of power, they were more of the type that makes the guys standing on the wall think twice before intruding (and protect themselves).

The same as Roberto Carlos's and Robin Van Persie but he didn't move very far away from the ball like the first, or have low conversion rate like the second. It was a great pleasure watching Batistuta play at his peak.

Reliability and Persistence

Guess who's Argentina's all-time top scorer?

No, he's not Di Stefano, Maradona, or Messi. It's Gabriel Omar Batistuta with 56 goals in 78 games (a better conversion rate than Messi, the second, who has 49 goals in 107 games).

Batitsuta was one of the best attackers to ever play soccer, and the best among them ever according to Maradona. Not only because of the goals he scored, but because he did all this while playing almost alone in Fiorentina.

Unlike Ronaldo, Messi, or Van Basten, Batitstuta rarely had plenty of world class players working by his side, except when played for Argentina.

When he was later asked, why he refused to leave Fiorentina when the club relegated in 1993, and join any of the other big clubs competing for him, he said he would prefer to win titles the "hard" way in Florence rather than win easy titles in Real Madrid or Manchester United.

He then said: *"One title with Fiorentina is worth ten with Milan or Juventus."*

Batistuta was the type of players who liked to challenge his own self, and always faced them with power and persistence.

He might have not won many trophies but he was a great player to be called by a legend like Maradona as the best attacker he had ever seen playing the beautiful game.

Zlatan Ibrahimović – Il Genio (The Genius)

Full Name: Zlatan Ibrahimović
Date of birth: 3 October 1981
Nationality: Swedish
Status: Still active
Clubs: Malmö (Sweden) - Ajax (Netherland) - Juventus, Inter Milan, AC Milan (Italy) - Barcelona (Spain) – PSG (France)
Goals scored and number of games: 419 goals in 748 games and counting
Goals scored internationally: 62 goals in 111 Caps
Club trohpies:
Note: Ibrahimović is the only player in this book who won the league title with 6 different teams in 4 different countries.

- The Dutch league (Erdivisie): Twice 2001–02, 2003–04 (Ajax)
- The Italian League (Serie A): 6 times 2004–05, 2005–06 (Juventus) - 2006–07, 2007–08, 2008–09 (Inter Milan) - 2010–11 (AC Milan)
- The Spanish League (La Liga): 2009–10 (Barcelona)
- The French League (League 1): 4 times 2012–13, 2013–14, 2014–15 - 2015-2016 (PSG is currently leading the league table with 19 points above Monco the second).
- The Dutch Cup: 2001–02
- The French Cup: 2014–15
- UEFA Super Cup: 2009 (Barcelona)
- FIFA Club World Cup: 2009 (Barcelona)
- The Italian Super Cup: 3 times 2006, 2008 (Inter Milan) – 2011 (AC Milan)
- The Spanish Super Cup: Twice (2009 – 2010)

- The French Super Cup: 3 times (2013 – 2014 – 2015)
- The French League Cup: Twice (2013–14, 2014–15)

National team trophies:

None, but Ibra is Sweden's All-time top goal-scorer and in 2012 Ibra received his "own" verb in the Swedish dictionary (Zlatanera) which means: To Dominate

Personal trophies:

- FIFA Puskás Award (Best goal of the year award): Received it in 2013 for his miraculous bicycle-kick goal against England.
- Best player in Italy: Twice 2009 and 2012
- Ligue 1 Player of the Year: Twice 2012–13, 2013–14
- Serie A Soccerer of the Year: 3 times 2008, 2009 (Inter Milan) and 2011 (AC Milan)
- Best Swedish soccer player: 10 times 2005, 2007, 2008, 2009, 2010, 2011, 2012, 2013, 2014, 2015
- Swedish Male Athlete of the Year: 4 times (2008 – 2010 – 2013 – 2015)
- PSG's all-time goal scorer with 123 goals in 147 games (He's currently leading the French league scoring table with 18 goals in 20 games).

Career Overview

In the first of October 1981, Zlatan Ibrahimović was born as the fifth kid for a Bosnian emigrant, who escaped to Sweden in 1970, and a Croatian mother who lost her custody of her youngest son at the age of 9.

Having to deal with his alcoholic father time and time again, Ibrahimović found his haven outside home, on the streets of Rosengård, were he learned what it took to be a young adult in one of the poorest districts in Sweden.

In addition to getting himself in lots and lots of problems, one of which was robbery, the time he spent on the streets gave him the opportunity to develop a special relationship with the ball.

Unlike the rest of the kids, most of young Ibra's time was spent on watching and imitating other soccer players, which later gave him the chance, along with his strong physique, to join the youth team of FF Malmo.

In Malmo, he drew all the attention to him, despite being buzzed by his teammates for being selfish and keeping the ball in his possession for too long rather than give an easy pass.

One story about him at that time was when the team was 4 goals behind and he came in early in the second half to score 8 goals in less than 30 minutes.

This got him a place in the youth team at Malmo where he scored 13 goals in 28 games during his first full season with the Swedish team.

To Amsterdam

Ibrahimović's performance at Malmo caught the eyes of many European teams including Arsenal whose people asked the young Swedish to spend 3 weeks with them to see how good he was to join the English Champion at that time.

But to their huge surprise, he declined their offer telling them that he doesn't do "auditions" before he later joined Ajax Amsterdam in July 2001.

In Ajax; Ibra spent his first few months as a backup striker for another young attacker called Mido, but sooner he managed to become his team's key attacker scoring 35 goals in 72 games.

One of those was in a league game against Breda when he scored a wonderful goal after playing with four defenders and their goalkeeper scoring one Ajax's remarkable goals.

Italy: Playing for The Big 3

In 2004; Juventus secured a deal with Ajax to buy their Swedish talent for 20 million dollars – a huge number for a young talent – and this was probably the tipping point of Ibra's career or the point where Ibra moved from being a very good player to an exceptional one.

This was all because of the club's manager Fabio Capello who realized that it wasn't perfect for Ibrahimović to waste his talent, physical strength and hovering around the ball away from the penalty area but rather he must redefine his role on the field to stick more to the box and become more effective.

So, under the eyes of Capello and his assistants; Ibra's training routine were doubled and he was kept late after each training session to practice his new role in the field.

And it did pay off and Ibra was the team's key attacker, scoring 23 goals in 69 games and helping the team win 2 consecutive league titles.

But the "Calciopoli" which resulted in Juventus being relegated to the second division made him refuse to stay with the team like Pavel Nedved, Gianluigi Buffon, and Alessandro Del Piero and move to Inter Milan in summer 2006 for a deal of 29 million dollars.

With Inter; Ibra proved how he was worth those 29 million scoring 66 goals in 3 seasons helping the team win 3 consecutive league titles and securing the 2008-09 golden boot for himself with 25 goals in hand.

Achieving The Dream in Barcelona

Ibra joined Barcelona in 2009 to fulfill one of his earliest dreams however the presence of players like Messi, Iniesta and Xavi Hernandez.

The lack of communication between him and Barça's coach at that time – Pep Guardiola – who refused to play Zlatan in his favorite position as a center forward.

Before forcing for a move in 2010 to AC Milan where he found himself again and helped the Italian giants win their first league title since 2004, scoring 14 goals during his first season with them before becoming the Serie-A's top goal scorer the next year after scoring 28 goals in 32 games.

After selling Paris Saint- Germain for the Qatari billionaire Nasser Al-Khelaifi, the chairman of Qatar Sports Investments, the French team believed they need to build their attacking line from scratch.

That's when they decided to sign Ibrahimović from Milan in 2012 so he can help the Parisian team win their first league title since 1994 and they got what they wanted the same year, as he helped them win not only one league title but 4, including the title of 2016 season.

Ibra is also managed to become the team's top goal scorer of all times after scoring 147 goals in 173 games (and counting).

Performance

Ibra can do everything, shooting with both feet – check, passing – check, heading – check, dribbling – check and the list goes one…

Powerful Volleys

Everything about Ibrahimović speaks power, from the way he carries himself to the way he reacts to defenders when they try to tease him.

The ex-taekwondo player who came from the tough neighborhood of Rosengård takes power as his motto on and off the field, and volleys is part of this.

Ibrahimović is one of the best players in soccer today who can shoot from almost anywhere on the playing field.

His physical strength (1.95m) as well as his strong foot enables him to direct the ball to wherever he wants no matter where he stands on the field and his goal against Anderlecht in the Champions league and his remarkable bicycle kick against England make the perfect demonstration to what I'm talking about.

Heels of Gold

I can't recall any player who uses his heels to score goals the way Ibrahimović does, he's the only player I know who scored back-heel goals with every team he played for including Sweden with which he scored an amazing goal in the world cup against Italy's Buffon.

Not only this new style made it difficult for the men marking him since they're now marking someone who can score even with his back facing the ball, but also it reinvented a new technique of scoring that added to the modern game.

Now every young kid is watching and imitating Ibra's moves from videos on YouTube but early in the 80s and 90s such technique wasn't dominant in soccer.

Myself, the only 2 goals I recall after years of watching soccer are Rabah Madjer's equalizer for Porto against Bayern Munich in the 1987 European cup final, and Thierry Henry's goal with Arsenal against Charlton, other than these two, no player has ever been known to score that amount of goals with the back of his foot like Ibrahimović.

Probably the most important of them all was against Atalanta in May 2009 when he needed a goal to become the league's top scorer only 5 minutes before the end of the final game and from a dead ball, he gave his back to Atalanta's goalkeeper and scored a back-heel that put him one goal ahead of Udenese's attacker, Antonio Di Natale.

Technical Skills

"He's done so many hours training by himself. That's why he became good". - One of Ibra's coaches in Malmo FF.

With lots of family problems and many attitude issues, Ibrahimović found his best friend at the ball he used to dangle for hours each day on the streets of Rosengård where he lived.

That gave him the ability to improve his ability to dribble and maintain full control over the ball despite his large size and this made him also one of the few attackers who combine between both, the extreme power and the effective dribbling skills.

His desire to be the very best on the field made dribbling for him become a challenge or a way to show his dominance over other players and he was so good at it that it became part of the player he is today.

When being asked about him sometimes refusing to pass to his teammates despite being in better positions than him he said his famous quote:

I like to dribble. So instead of passing, I sometimes choose to dribble instead. Sometimes my teammates get mad at me but that's just how things are. It's part of the game, it's no fun if you can't dribble. Soccer is supposed to be fun. If it's not, then what is the point?

Dominance and The Desire to Win

Only a few of players nowadays a coach can build an entire team around them. Ibrahimović is one of these players.

With the desire to win, the cocky attitude and the willingness to stay fit despite age. Every soccer fan wishes Ibrahimović becomes a player in his team no matter how much they likes or dislikes him personally. Trophies go wherever he goes.

In soccer, some coaches lack the ability to motivate their players. They may be good at tactics or the ability to keep faith in their players however, they don't win a lot unless they have the type of leaders in the team who can fire up the dressing room and get their teammates bleed and sweat for the shirt they're wearing.

Ibrahimović is one of these natural born leaders. He has this type of dominant personality, and the - somehow inflated - ego that pushes him to strive for greatness and more wins.

He can transform a team of average players into winners by just existing on the field, the same way he did with AC Milan in 2010.

Pele - The Gasoline

Full Name: Edson Arantes do Nascimento
Date of birth: 23 October 1940
Nationality: Brazilian
Status: Retired in 1977
Clubs: Santos (Brazil) - New York Cosmos (USA)
Goals scored and number of games: 1247 goals in 1335 games
Goals scored internationally: 95 goals in 113 Caps
Club trophies:
- Brazilian league (With Santos): 6 times (1961, 1962, 1963, 1964, 1965 and 1968)
- Paulistão or Brazilian league of São Paulo (With Santos): 10 times (1958, 1960, 1961, 1962, 1964, 1965, 1967, 1968, 1969 and 1973)
- Copa Libertadores (With Santos):: Twice 1962, 1963
- Intercontinental Cup (With Santos):: Twice 1962, 1963
- Intercontinental Super Cup (With Santos):: One time 1968
- North American Soccer League - equivalent to the current MLS – (With NY Cosmos): One time (1977)

National team trophies:
- The only player to win the FIFA World Cup 3 times: 1958, 1962, 1970

Personal trophies:
- FIFA Player of the Century: 2000
- The FIFA Order of Merit (The highest honor awarded by FIFA): 1984
- FIFA Ballon d'Or (prize of honor): 2013

- FIFA World Cup Best Player: 1970
- FIFA World Cup Best Young Player: 1958
- FIFA World Cup All-Star Team: 1958, 1970
- Best player in Copa America: 1959
- Copa America's top scorer: 1959
- Brazilian league's top scorer: 3 times (1961, 1963, 1964)
- Paulistão's top scorer: 11 times (1957, 1958, 1959, 1960, 1961, 1962, 1963, 1964, 1965, 1969, 1973)
- Top scorer of Copa Libertadores (1965)

Career Overview

Pele; who received his first shoe at the age of twelve started his relationship with soccer playing in the alleys of Tres Coracoes in Brazil before joining Bauru Atletico before joining Santos in 1956 to start an amazingly successful journey with the team he wore his shirts for 18 consecutive years.

Where Did The Name Come from?

Pele's father; " Dondinho" who was an attacking player for both Atletico Mineiro and Bauru Atletico before he was forced to retire because of a major ligament damage was inspired by the great inventor; Thomas Edison so he decided to name his son Edison.

But during school, he failed to pronounce the name of his favorite goalkeeper "Bilé" who played for Vasco da Gama which made the other kids make fun of him and call him Pele and since then, Edison became the Pele we know.

Pele's relationship with soccer started in the alleys of Tres Coracoes in Brazil before joining Bauru Atletico and Santos. There, his coach and the famous player who played in the 1934 world cup in Bauru "Waldemar de Brito" took the 15-year old Pele to Santos and told them that they should sign "the best player in the world".

That was the beginning of an amazingly successful journey with the team he wore his shirts for 18 consecutive years. In Santos he played with the youth team, scoring an outstanding number of 148 goals in 33 games.

This helped him join the first team, making his debut in 1956 in a 7-1 game against Corinthians.

He also made his first international debut and scored against Argentina in July 1957 one year before he travelled to Sweden with the team to help Brazil win their first world cup title after scoring six important goals including 3 goals against France which made him the youngest player in the world to score a hat-trick in the world cup.

He then helped Brazil defeat Sweden in the final game after scoring 2 goals in the game that ended 5-2 for the South Americans.

1962-1966: Titles and Injuries

After his first game against Mexico – in which he scored – Pele suffered from a major injury against Czechoslovakia in group stage.

Unfortunately this injury forced Pele to miss the entire tournament and watch his teammates; Garrincha, Zagalo and Vava secure Brazil's and Pele's second world cup title.

They could win the third in 1966 however; talented Pele became the target for every defender and receiving a huge number of kicks and tackles during his first game against Bulgaria (in which he scored to be the first player to score in 3 consecutive world cups).

This forced him not to play against Hungary which won the game by 3-1 before getting injured in another loss against Portugal to leave the world cup from the group stage and decide that he would never play again in the world cup after what happened to him.

However, his love for Brazil forced him to finally agree to play in the 1970 world cup qualifiers and in summer 1970; he made Brazil the world champion after scoring a header, before making his third and fourth assists in the tournament and helping Brazil defeat Italy 4-1 and win the world cup.

From Santos to New York Cosmos

After scoring his goal number 1000 with Santos in 1969 and after spending 18 years in Brazil, Pele decided to leave the team in 1974 before joining the American team one year later, scoring 64 goals in 107 games before retiring in 1977.

Performance

Pele is considered to be the undisputed number one striker ever, he had it all, and he also proved it with the long list of awards and trophies...

Artistic

Pele is praised frequently for being a goal-scoring machine however, only a few mention that he was also a technical genius, an artist, and a player with so many tricks up to his sleeves.

Being trained from a very young age by a professional soccerer, his father, got him to develop a unique connection with the ball and it always went to wherever he wanted it to go.

Probably the best demonstration for this wasn't a goal he scored but rather, a goal that he missed in the 1970 world cup against Uruguay.

A through pass was heading towards him while the Uruguayan keeper was also out for the ball, and rather than play on the ball, Pele feinted with his body without even touching the ball and tricked the goalkeeper who neither got the ball nor prevented Pele from reaching it.

Pele was also the one of the few players, with Ronaldo and Ronaldinho, to introduce new tricks to soccer one of which was the famous hat trick he did against Sweden in the final of the 1958 world cup.

Inside the penalty area and while being surrounded by 3 Swedish defenders, Pele raised the ball above one defender, waited for the ball to go down – making a shape of a curve or a hat – and then smashed it into the net.

At that time, tricks like this one were only made in Brazil, and probably this was the reason why Pele and Santos made scores against some of the biggest European clubs whenever the 2 clubs met.

Félix Venerando ,Pele's former teammate in the Brazilian team, said about his tricks: Pele was always several seconds ahead of the rest of us, when you stop to think about what he would do next, he's already done it.

Excellent Shooting Skills

Some people say Pele was an overrated player who played at times when soccer was a lot easier and less tactical than how it is today.

This can be true however, one can't score 1284 goals without having a set of special skills allowing him to score that gigantic number of goals.

Despite the fact that the game was not as complicated as it is today, only Pele managed to score this number of goals, and the major thing that helped him to do so was his excellent finish.

Each of Pele's feet were equally lethal and because he was only 5 ft. 8 in, he could easily generate enough power to make his shots dangerous without needing lots of space for preparation.

The last goal of his hat-trick against France in the 1958 world cup describe this perfectly, he received the ball outside the box, the ball was jumpy because grounds back then weren't as smooth as the ones we see today yet he managed to control the ball and smashed it beautifully inside the French net without the need to look at the goal as if his right foot know where the goal was which is true indeed.

A Master in The Air

Despite not being super tall, Pele was extraordinary in air plays, he had style, his jumps were well crafted and he could hit the ball with both accuracy and power towards wherever he wanted it to go.

He wasn't the tallest or the strongest inside the penalty area yet he knew how to position himself well and had right jumping technique to help him do what he wanted or in the words of one of his teammates: He got the calculations right.

The highlight of Pele's career can be summed in two famous incidents, both of them in the 1970 world cup. The second was against Italy in the final when he scored against the legend Dino Zoff.

The best thing about this goal was Pele's ability to create power and momentum for his jump from stability and without moving towards the ball. It came slightly behind him yet he knew how to generate power and aim it perfectly towards Italy's goal in a deadly place against a world class goalkeeper.

The best of his headers however, was his header against England in the group stages of the same tournament which is frequently used in any goalkeeping saves compilation on YouTube.

He received a cross from Carlos Alberto, and with excellent form he hit the ball from the penalty spot towards the ground so it jumps and tricks the English goalkeeper, Gordon Banks.

This ball was so difficult for any goalkeeper to save to the extent that it was later chosen as the best save in the history of the world cup and one of the best 10 saves in soccer in the 20th century.

Gerd Muller - Der Bomber (The Smasher

Full Name: Gerhard Müller

Date of birth: 3 November 1945

Nationality: German

Status: Retired (1981)

Clubs: 1861 Nördlingen, Bayern Munich - Fort Lauderdale Strikers (USA)

Goals scored and number of games: 723 goals in 771 games

Goals scored internationally: 68 goals in 62 Caps (A world record)

Club Trophies:

-   UEFA Champions League (European Cup): 3 Consecutive Times (FC Bayern)
-   European Cup Winners' Cup: 1966 - 67 (FC Bayern)
-   Intercontinental Cup: 1976 (FC Bayern)
-   German League (Bundesliga): 4 Times (FC Bayern)
-   German Cup: 4 Times (FC Bayern)

National team trophies:

-   FIFA World Cup: Gold Medal 1974
-   UEFA European Championship: Gold Medal 1972

Personal trophies:

-   FIFA World Cup Golden Boot: 1970 (third best goal scoring record: 14 goals)
-   Ballon d'Or: 1970
-   German Soccerer of the Year: Twice
-   Bundesliga top scorer: 6 times
-   15th in World Soccer Magazine's greatest 100 players of all times

Career Overview

Born in a small town that was ruined by the world war, Gerhard Müller started playing soccer at the age of 7 with his friends on the streets of the Bavarian town, Nördlingen.

At the age of 9 he witnessed one of the most memorable acts in the history of soccer which was later to be known as "The Miracle of Bern" when West Germany defeated the strong Hungarian team, the Mighty Magyars, and won the world cup in 1954.

Not only that world cup inspired Muller to become a soccerer, it also affected his playing style and finishing skills which he got from the world's best attacker at that time, Ferenc Puskás.

At the age of 18, and after spending 3 years in their youth team, Muller made his debut with 1861 Nördlingen to score a remarkable record of 51 goals in 31 games which brought attention to him and got many clubs to approach him for his signature before the end of his first season with Nördlingen.

Yet he chose to wait until summer wishing he would eventually receive an offer from Norenberg, the team he insanely supported, however, it didn't happen so he chose to join a small team in Bavaria playing in the German second division under the name of Bayern Munich.

Making History in Bavaria

When talking about the history of the great Bayern Munich, we can divide it into 2 eras, before Gerd Muller, and after Gerd Muller.

Simply, and honestly, without Gerd Muller we would never have seen the trophy-winning machine we know today under the name of FC Bayern, the team that had only won two domestic cups in 64 years before the coming of Muller, and moved on to become Germany's most successful team with 25 league titles and 5 European cups.

Since he promoted with the club to the German 1st division, the Bundesliga, Bayern's performance improved dramatically, and finished third on their first year in the division before winning the league in 1969 for the first time in 38 years, followed by 3 consecutive titles in between 1972 and 1974. And the top scorer for the 4 competitions was Muller.

Dominating Europe

Now that the club has established itself as a super power in Germany, it was time for Muller, Franz Beckenbauer, Uli Hoeness, and the newcomer, Karl-Heinz Rummenigge to prove themselves among the biggest teams in Europe.

Between 1973 and 1976 when Bayern Munich won the European Cup for 3 times in a row after defeating Atletico Madrid, Leeds United, and Saint-Étienne respectively, thanks to the performance of Muller who scored twice against Madrid and once against Leeds United.

Die Mannschaft

Muller's journey with the West German team witnessed one of the most respected performances for an international player.

With a world record that exceeded one goal per international game (68 goals in 62 Caps), Muller helped West Germany to establish itself as a soccer super power in Europe after almost 2 decades since the last time they won their last major championship in 1954.

In only 8 years with the national team, Muller became Germany's all-time top scorer, and helped the team win two world cup medals, including a gold on in 1974 when they defeated Netherlands in the final game in Munich two years after scoring twice in West Germany's 3-0 win against the Soviet Union in the 1972 European Championship.

Despite these successes, and his 14-goals' record in the world cup, Muller announced his international retirement one week after winning the world cup regarding some problems with the German soccer federation.

Retirement

After 15 years in Bavaria, Muller – 34 years at the time – decided to move to America to join Fort Lauderdale Strikers with which he scored 38 goals in two and a half years with the club.

However, a problem with alcohol started to emerge and he decided to move back in Germany to receive help from his best friends in Bayern Beckenbauer, Hoeness who helped him quit and offered him a managerial job in the team he served sincerely for more than a decade.

Performance Overview

Muller was the king of 18 yard box, as soon as he entered it you knew that a goal was approaching.

The smasher, der Bomber

If there is a list for the best finishers in the history of soccer, Gerd Muller would be among its top 3. Simply, no one can reach a goal scoring rate of 0.98 – almost a goal per game – and have more international goals than his games with the German team - 68 goals in 62 games – including 14 goals in the World Cup, without being exceptional in front of the goal.

Muller's ruthlessness in front of the goal was the thing that convinced his coach at Bayern Munich, Zlatko Čajkovski who had previously announced he was too fat to play soccer, to admit his ignorance and give Muller the opportunity to become FC Bayern's key attacker.

What was his technique though?

"When I got the ball, I smashed it in." Gerd Muller

This was his philosophy. Without acting stylish or trying to demonstrate his skills, he just mimicked his childhood hero, Ferenc Puskás, and knew that power makes all the difference when being inside the box.

Excellent pace for a short player

Like I previously mentioned, Muller didn't look like a traditional attacker and didn't seem to be physically equipped to play alone at the front.

He wasn't perceived as a fast player either yet he had something more important than speed which is acceleration, and for a center forward, the later was more important than the former.

Why? Because speed wasn't important for anyone playing at a close distance from the goalkeeper, what's more important is the one-seconded, quick, acceleration the attacker needs to move from stability so he can create space for himself to shoot the ball.

Like Messia, Maradona, and the majority of short players, Muller's physique (1.76m) allowed him to be relatively close to the ground and move faster since his short feet enabled to accelerate faster than his peers.

This why he was able to beat goalkeepers easily in 1-on-1 situations and was also the reasons why he could escape defenders so easily.

Simply look at his equalizer against Netherlands in the world cup final and watch how he escaped three Dutch defenders inside the penalty area by only adjusting his movement so quickly to keep them off balance and score the goal.

A high portion of smartness

Muller was unique at the way he used what he had to create sever danger to his opponents, he could literally predict where the ball would go, as if he had a sensor in his brain, and he would always prepare himself to receive the ball at its next position before it's even played to him.

His second goal against Italy in the world cup semifinal and his goal in the same year against Leeds United in the European cup final were both similar and ordinary.

The first was a header passed to him and he met it with his head in the Italian net and the second was a crossed-pass which he ruthlessly directed with his foot.

The execution might have seemed ordinary but the way he moved to meet the ball before he scored it was magnificent. In both crucial goals, Muller has started his movement way before the ball was even passed, as if he knew where the ball will go and he got what he had worked for.

Ruud Van Nistelrooy –

Van Gol

Full Name: Rutgerus Martinus van Nistelrooy

Date of birth: 1 July 1976

Nationality: Dutch

Status: Retired (2012)

Clubs: Den Bosch, Heerenveen, PSV Eindhoven (Netherlands) - Real Madrid, Malaga (Spain) - Manchester United (England) - Hamburg SV (Germany)

Goals scored and number of games: 382 goals in 659 games

Goals scored internationally: 35 goals in 70 Caps

Club Trophies: With Clubs:

- English Premier League: 2002–03
- Spanish League (La Liga): Twice (Real Madrid)
- Dutch League (Eredivisie): Twice (PSV Eindhoven)
- English Cup (FA Cup): 2003–04
- English League Cup: 2005–06
- English Super Cup (FA Community Shield): 2003
- Spanish Super Cup (Supercopa de España): 2008 (Real Madrid)
- Dutch Super Cup: Twice (PSV Eindhoven)

National team trophies:

None

Personal trophies:

- Pele's List for the greatest 100 soccerers of all times.
- Spanish League Golden Boot (The Pichichi): 2006–07
- Premier League Golden Boot: 2002–03
- Dutch League Golden Boot: Twice

- UEFA Champions League Top Scorer: Three times
- English Player of the year: Twice
- Dutch Soccerer of the Year: Twice

Career Overview

Despite not spending much in Manchester United, I believe Ruud Van Nistelrooy is among the top 5 attackers who ever played for the club that dominated the English soccer for more than 20 years under the reign of Alex Ferguson.

Van Nistelrooy started his career in Den Bosch, the local team that has made a massive surprise when they reached the final game of the 1991 Dutch Cup.

His performance got him join the first team at the age of 17 and maintain a consistent place at the first squad.

However, finishing 7th in the Eerste Divisie – division two – got him to move up to SC Heerenveen with which he only spent one year before grabbing the attention of the giants, PSV Eindhoven, who were in the market for a striker to help them regain the league title they lost to Ajax in 1998.

PSV

Van Nistelrooy didn't need so much time to adapt in Eindhoven, and made one of his best performances in 1998 when he scored 38 goals in 46 games, that got him on top of the league scoring list, and helped his team win their third Dutch super cup in a row.

The following year however, was more glorious as he, despite being injured for 2 months, helped Eindhoven win their 15th league title after scoring 29 goals in only 23 games which, again, made him the Eredivisie top scorer and the Dutch soccerer of the year 2000.

Such performance grabbed the attention of Sir Alex Ferguson who approached PSV with a $24 deal that was accepted by the player yet a strong injury late in 2000 threatened to cancel the deal as Nistelrooy spent the entire year in the hospital and was forced to pass another, medical test before the deal was completed in summer 2001.

Manchester United

It didn't take the Dutch player time to prove himself in England. He first came second, only one goal, behind Thierry Henry in the league's scoring list, before scoring 10 goals in 14 European games to help United reach the semifinal however, they lost, on goal difference, to Bayer Leverkusen which qualified to play against the champion, Real Madrid.

The following year was even better, as he helped United win their 15th league title and was top scorer for both the Champions League and the premier league with 44 goals he scored in 2003.

Ruud then continued his top performance with the club, yet problems with the rising star, Cristiano Ronaldo, forced Alex Ferguson to interfere by accepting Real Madrid's $19 million offer in summer 2006.

That year, and before he joined Madrid, Nistelrooy made one of the most hilarious celebrations in modern soccer on the day Netherlands met Andora in the 2006 world cup qualifications.

He was first laughed by one of Andora's defenders after missing a penalty, yet, a few minutes later, and after he scored the fourth goal of the game, he marched towards that defender and waved his hands hilariously right in front of him.

The Real Madrid Era

In Madrid, Nistelrooy proved himself as one of the most successful, and rare, deals in the Galacticos era as he won the Pichichi award just on his first season in Spain, scoring 25 league goals, and helping Madrid win the league for the first time since 2003, before helping adding a second title the following year thanks to his 16 league goals.

Nistelrooy then suffered a set of injuries during his last 2 years with Madrid as he only played 16 games during that period before he accepted a mid-season offer from Hamburg early in 2010 with which he spent 2 years before finishing his last year in soccer playing for Malaga as he helped the Spanish club qualify to the Champions league for the first time in their history after finishing fourth in the league in 2012.

Performance Overview

Van Nistelrooy was a classic striker, put him in the 18 yard box, and soon a goal is approaching.

Very powerful

Except for the period when both Cristiano Ronaldo and Wayne Rooney played together at the front, Manchester United rarely was the team who put amusement before winning. United would go an entire season winning games with only one goal difference and end up the champions.

They realistically considered winning before amusement, and that's why Alex Ferguson risked 20 million Euros – a huge number at that time – to buy the injured, yet physically powerful, Van Nistelrooy, who could score from half chances, no matter how strong the defense he was playing against.

The fact that United's playing style at that time depended on sending long balls and crosses to the man upfront required a special type of attackers who was both strong, and can keep the ball close to him in crowded areas, and this was exactly what Nistelrooy was good at.

The Dutch attacker was one of the best players in receiving the ball with his back facing the goal. He knew how to use his body to keep the ball around despite being chased by defenders and he rarely lost a fight for the ball both on the ground and in the air.

The sequence of receive, turn and hit was Van Nistelrooy's mark in the great majority of his goals in United. He would receive the cross, hold on to the ball, then turn and strike the ball with his strong right foot.

High conversion rate

Like I said earlier, Alex Ferguson needed an attacker who could score from half chances or less, and by comparing his number of goals with the number of shots he had on and off-target, anyone will realize how valuable Nistelrooy was to Manchester United.

Since he arrived to England in 2001, Nistelrooy maintained one of the highest conversion rates in the history of the English Premier League with 71% conversion rate per season which reached 84% in 2002-03, the same season he scored 44 goals in 52 games for United.

Quite similar to Romario, Nistelrooy was the type of attackers who could stay motionless for a full 80 minutes then scores a double before the game ends.

His shot accuracy was amazing and he would never rush a shot if he wasn't sure of it hitting the net. I believe if he would've broken many records if he was to stay with Manchester United rather than leave to Madrid.

Wayne Rooney - Wazza

Full Name: Wayne Mark Rooney
Date of birth: 24 October 1985
Nationality: English
Status: Currently playing for Manchester United
Clubs: Everton, Manchester United (England)
Goals scored and number of games: 312 goals in 699 games
Goals scored internationally: 51 goals in 109 Caps (and counting)
Club Trophies:
- UEFA Champions League: 2007–08 (Manchester United)
- FIFA Club World Cup: 2008 (Manchester United)
- English Premier League: 5 Times (Manchester United)
- English League Cup: Twice (Manchester United)
- English Super Cup (FA Community Shield): Three Times (Manchester United)

Personal trophies:
- English young player of the year: Twice
- English player of the year: 2009–10
- FIFA Club World Cup Golden Ball: 2008
- Manchester United player of the year: Twice
- Premier League all-time goal scorers: Second after Alan Shearer (191 goals in 425 games)

Career Overview

Wayne Rooney quickly established himself in the English soccer when he pulled a stunner from a long distance in Everton's 2-1 win against Arsenal, only 5 days before celebrating his 17th birthday, to stop the league champions' record of 30 consecutive games without a single defeat.

That goal made Rooney the youngest player to ever score a goal in the history of the Premier League and helped Everton, alongside with his other 5 goals, to finish 7th on the 2002-03 league table.

Rooney continued to be part of David Moyes's squad for the second year in a row and was given the chance to appear in 34 league games in which he scored 9 goals, six of which were scored near the end of the season and helped Everton finish one place above the relegation area.

That performance lured different teams to approach Rooney, including Arsenal and Newcastle United whose $25 million offer was rejected by Everton's executive yet they found it hard to resist Alex Ferguson's bid for $32 million which made Rooney the most expensive youngster in the history of the English soccer.

This transfer record stood still for 14 years until Manchester United signed the 19 year-old Anthony Martial from AS Monaco in a $45 million deal.

Manchester United

Despite winning nothing except the 2006 League Cup against Wigan, Rooney quickly established himself as a key player in United. He formed a strong duo with Ruud Van Nistelrooy with both of them scoring 77 goals in all competitions, including Van Nistelrooy's revenge against Arsenal in 2005 when he faked a penalty and scored a goal in United's 2-0 win that stopped Arsenal's long, unbeaten record at 49 consecutive games.

The following year however was transforming for Rooney and the English giants that have been missing on the league title for three consecutive years yet, and despite their famous fight in the 2006 world cup, a strong companionship was formed between Rooney and Cristiano Ronaldo.

This resulted in 153 goals, 3 consecutive league titles and 2 consecutive European finals including the famous win against Chelsea when John Terry slipped before taking the final penalty kick and gave united the chance to come back to the game and win their third major European title.

After Ronaldo

Everything changed in Manchester United except Rooney who continued to keep his form and stay United's key attacker when all other attacking options came and gone.

In the 2011 – 12 season Rooney was on the verge of winning his fifth league title with Manchester after scoring 27 goals, including his fantastic bicycle kick against Manchester City, and finishing second behind Arsenal's Robin Van Persie on the goal scoring list.

Yet United's strange loss of the lead after being 7 points above Man City sent the title towards the other side of the city the day when Sergio Aguero scored in the stoppage time in City's 3-2 win against Queens Park Rangers.

Post Ferguson Era

After forming another strong duo, but now with the newcomer, Robin Van Persie, Rooney helped the United players say goodbye to Alex Ferguson in a special way after winning the club's 20th league title, and the 13th under Ferguson's reign, in the 2012-13 season.

A month later, Rooney was approached by both Arsenal and Chelsea, yet he chose to stay with United and train with the new coach, David Moyes, the guy who gave him the opportunity to play in Everton when he was young.

Unfortunately, Moyes's period with United was unsuccessful and many players left the team, including Van Persie, yet Rooney chose to stay with the club and be part of Luis Van Gaal's current squad.

Performance Overview

Rooney can score from anywhere at any time. Just put him close to the 18 yard box, and you can be pretty much sure that a goal is approaching.

He could play anywhere

Rooney played as a second attacker next to Van Nistelrooy, a lone attacker in front of Ronaldo, a winger next to Van Persie, and a playmaker behind him and Falcao,

Rooney's ability to adapt since he joined Manchester United coming from Everton in 2004 was impressive and still being one of the best things that identify him as a great player.

Unlike many attackers who would suffer outside the box, Rooney was both technically and tactically gifted to the extent that he was once being played by Luis Van Gaal in the defensive midfield when Michael Carrick was absent.

He sometimes hated it, especially with the Dutch manager, yet being able to perform well at many, many times made him a player you could hardly let go, and one of the highest paid players in the English soccer.

Excellent shooting power

I'm someone who enjoys to watch the ball being struck from a distance and tear the net apart, I love seeing attackers scoring from distances.

It gives my butterflies, and it's probably the reason why me, the huge arsenal fan, considers Wayne Rooney as one of my best soccer players, not just because he scores A LOT, but because he has a variety of goal scoring skills only a few among his peers would ever have.

If we simply track the best 50 goals scored in England in the past 20 years, we'd easily find some of them tagged under "Wayne Rooney".

From his marvelous goal against Newcastle United when he one-touched a ball from Newcastle's defender to struck a 25-yard volley to the right corner of Shay Given's goal, to the outstanding bicycle kick he scored against Manchester City 12 minutes before the end of the Manchester derby at Old Trafford.

Fast

Like Gerd Muller, Rooney is short, thick, with excellent agility that allows him to beat the toughest of defenders.

Despite not looking like a player who could run a 100 meters in 10 seconds or less, Rooney's physique and body composition allows him to stay close to the ball, giving him the chance to dribble past defenders very quickly, add to it his toned body and you get an attacker you could hardly beat.

The run he made with the ball against Charlton Athletic in 2005 is still being remembered as one of the best team goals for Manchester United since they started the Premier League.

He received the ball 7 yards before the center, ran the entire half while dribbling past 3 players before sending a chipped ball to Van Nistelrooy who received the ball, before turning and striking it from inside the box.

Nistelrooy still considers this goal as the best he scored with Manchester and one of the best in his career, not for his strong finish but for the effort 18 year-old Rooney has put in the play.

Hernan Crespo –
Valdanito

Full Name: Hernán Jorge Crespo

Date of birth: 5 July 1975

Nationality: Argentine

Status: Retired (2012), and currently managing Modena FC

Clubs: Parma, Lazio, Inter Milan, Genoa, Milan (Italy) - River Plate (Argentina) - Chelsea (England)

Goals scored and number of games: 306 goals in 672 games

Goals scored internationally: 35 goals in 64 Caps (and counting)

Club Trophies:

- UEFA Cup: 1998–99 (Parma)
- Copa Libertadores: 1996
- Italian League (Serie A): Three Times (Inter Milan)
- English Premier League: 2005–06
- Argentine League(Apertura): Twice
- Italian Cup (Coppa Italia): 1998–99 (Parma)
- Italian Super Cup (Supercoppa Italiana): 5 Times (Parma, Lazio, Milan, Inter)
- English Super Cup (FA Community Shield): 2005

International Trophies:

- Silver Medal at Olympic Games 1996

Personal trophies:

- Pele's List for the greatest 100 soccerers of all times.
- 2006 FIFA World Cup: Silver Boot
- Serie A Top Scorer (Capocannoniere trophy): 2000–01
- Argentine League top scorer: 1994

- Summer Olympics top goal scorer: 1996

Career Overview

Crespo started his professional career early in Argentina when he made his debut with the giants, River Plate, at the age of 18 and quickly got himself a place in the first team with the 11 goals he scored in the Apertura which got them finish second on the league table, only 3 points behind Club Independiente.

The highlight, however, of Crespo's career with River Plate came in 1996, when he helped Ramón Díaz's team, with his 10 championship goal, to win the Copa Libertadoras title for the second time in their history after scoring River Plate's 2 goals their two-legged win against the third most successful team in Colombia, America de Cali.

With that performance, it wasn't strange to grab the attention of multiple European clubs, and despite an interest from AS Roma, Crespo chose to join Parma and their talented team that had legends like Gianluigi Buffon, Dino Baggio, Fabio Canavaro, Lilian Thuram and Juan Sebastián Verón,.

In Parma, and despite failing to score a single goal in any of his first 6 appearances, Crespo ended his first season in Italy scoring 12 goals which were the beginning to later become the club's all-time goal scorer.

In fact, he was so close to help the team make their first Calcio title ever after finishing second, only two points behind Juventus.

He then scored another 12 league goals the following year before making one of his best performances ever in 1998-99, and make contribution to 37 goals that resulted in the most successful season in Parma's history.

The same year that witnessed them winning 3 titles, the Italian Cup against Batistuta's Fiorentina - he scored twice - the UEFA Cup against Marseille – he scored once – and the Italian Super cup in which he scored Parma's equalizer in their 2-1 win against AC Milan.

In 2000 though, Crespo left Parma to join Lazio at a transfer record of 35 million Euros.

It wasn't just for money, in fact, Lazio had some of the best players in Europe and the world wearing his shirt and has won both the Italian league and the UEFA Super cup the year before.

It was an opportunity for Crespo to prove himself and be part of the team that had legends like Alessandro Nesta, Siniša Mihajlović, Pavel Nedved, Veron, Claudio Lopez and Diego Simeone.

He disappointed nobody actually, as he scored 28 goals on his first season, that made him Italy's capocannoniere, and allowed him to help the Rome-based team win the Italian Super cup title against Inter Milan, and finish 6 points behind the champions, Roma.

Italy and England, back and forth

Financial troubles caught Lazio in 2002 and forced to sell some of their best players to different rivals and in only two years, Lazio's fans watched their captain, Alessandro Nesta move to Milan, their number 9 Pavel Nedved join Juventus, and their best attacker, Crespo, join Inter Milan.

With Inter he spent an amazing half season and scored 9 times in 12 champion's league games yet he spent the second half of the season out for injury before moving to London to join Chelsea in their journey to win their first league titles in 50 years under the management of Claudio Ranieri.

In England, Crespo spent a good first year, scoring 10 league goals and finishing second behind Arsenal however, he decided to move back to Italy and join AC Milan on a loan deal to help the team reach the European final and score in the final which they dramatically lost to Liverpool in 2005.

Such disappointment got him to move back to Chelsea, and help the club, finally, win the league under the reign of Jose Mourniho whose total dependence on Didier Drogba forced Crespo to cut his contract and move to Inter Milan.

Back in Inter again, he helped the club win 3 league titles in a row. He then joined Genoa for half a year before cutting his contract and move to Parma to set the end of his love journey with the club which witnessed his retirement in 2012.

Performance Overview

Not the world's greatest dribbler or fastest runner, but excellent scoring abilities.

An air-play master

When it came to air plays, Crespo was one of the best. Being able to position himself properly when the cross arrived, Crespo scored some of his best goals from long passes, either by foot or with his head.

I recall his goal against Ajax Amsterdam as one of the best technically performed air play I've ever seen. A magnificent, banana-type, curvy cross by Christian Vieri, followed by a powerful jump that put Crespo above Ajax's defender to score a long header in Inter's 2-0 win in Amsterdam Arena.

A heavy left foot

Some people blamed Crespo for not using his right foot so often, but who needs a strong right foot when his left can do whatever he wanted it to do.

Despite spending most of his prime time in Parma and Lazio which didn't have the financial stamina to add more talents to their attacking power, Crespo scored some of Parma and Lazio's greatest goals ever using his left that had no mercy.

Like I said before, Crespo was a classic attacker who found air inside the box and didn't craft his goals around volleys and long shots, yet the one thing he had better than anybody else is his ability to use his left foot from almost any condition.

From back-heels, bicycle kicks, and shots on and off the ground, he could alter his position almost anywhere on and off the ground to score with his dominant, left foot.

I recall his first goal at Stamford Bridge with Chelsea when he scored against Fulham. He received a cross, and took a slight jump to hit the fast ball with his left. At first the goal seemed easy however it was very hard technically to target the fast ball that way, and with that power.

Miroslav Klose – Salto (somersault in German)

Full Name: Miroslav Josef Klose
Date of birth: 9 June 1978
Nationality: German
Status: Currently playing (S.S Lazio)
Clubs: SG Blaubach-Diedelkopf, FC 08 Homburg, Kaiserslautern, Werder Bremen, Bayern Munich (Germany) - Lazio (Italy)
Goals scored and number of games: 296 goals in 727 games
Goals scored internationally: 71 goals in 137 Caps (Top goal scorer)

Club Trophies:
- German League (Bundesliga): Twice (Bayern Munich)
- German Cup: Twice (Bayern Munich)
- Italian Cup (Coppa Italia): 2012–13
- German League Cup: Twice (Werder Bremen, Bayern Munich)
- German Super Cup: 2010 (Bayern Munich)

International trophies:
- FIFA World Cup: Gold Medal 2014
- FIFA World Cup: Silver Medal 2002
- FIFA World Cup: Bronze Medal 2006, 2010
- EURO 08: Silver Medal

Personal trophies:
- FIFA World Cup all-time record goal scorer (16 goals)
- The only player to win 4 World Cup medals
- FIFA World Cup: Golden Boot (2006)
- FIFA World Cup: Silver Boot (2002)
- German League top goal scorer: 2005–06

Career Overview

Klose, a Polish descendant who spent his early childhood in France as his father, a professional soccerer, was offered a three-year contract to join Auxerre FC which he later helped promote to the French first division after finishing first on the League 2 table in 1980.

As a full-time carpenter, Klose didn't consider soccer as his real job only when he made his first debut with Kaiserslautern's second team in 1998, the same year they won the German Bundesliga, before making his biggest impact with the team when he finished third on the league's scoring list only two goals behind 1860 München's Martin Max, and Borussia Dourtmund's attaker, Márcio Amoroso.

Such performance was admired by Germany's new manager, Rudi Voller, who decided to make Klose his key attacker in the 2002 world cup alongside the maven, Oliver Bierhoff, with which Klose has formed a strong duo, and helped Germany reach the final game with his 5 world cup goals that got him to joint-win the tournament's silver shoe with Rivaldo.

Despite the injury, Klose continued to score goals with Kaiserslautern until the year 2004 when the league champions, Werder Bremen, decided to reinforce their front line with Klose who quickly established himself as the star of the team.

That season Klose helped them win the German cup in 2006 and finish second on the league table behind Bayern Munich after finishing the season as the championship top scorer with 25 goals in 26 games.

And again, his impressive domestic performance got him the chance to be part of Germany's quest to win the 2006 world cup.

Despite failing to do so, Klose finished the tournament as Germany's top scorer, but this time he won the Golden Shoe after scoring 5 goals, including a late equalizer in the quarter final game against Argentina, which Germany won after a penalty shootout.

Bayern Munich

Now looking for domestic trophies, Klose decided it's time to play for a big team and try his luck winning the German league so he accepted Bayern Munich's offer, and helped the club win 2 league titles and reach the 2009-10 European final after scoring 9 times in Bayern's journey towards the final game against Chelsea.

During the 4 years he spent with the German giants, Klose won 6 domestic titles and scored 53 goals in 149 games one year after he helped Germany finish third in the 2010 world cup in which he scored 4 goals, including a habitual double against Argentina in Germany's 4-0 quarter-final win.

Lazio and World cup history

Looking for a new adventure, Klose decided to move to Italy and join Lazio in 2011.

That move was described by Klose himself as a "late move" as he later described that playing in Italy was unlike anywhere else in Europe, and used the incident when the post guy, a Lazio fan, knocked on his door the day before the derby against Rome in the Cup final, and begged him with tears in his eyes to do anything he could to prevent Roma from winning the title.

This later happened as Senad Lulić scored a late winner in the Olimpico Stadium to help Lazio win their 6th Coppa Italia title on the 26th of May 2013.

Performance Overview

Klose was never known for his dribbling skills, not either for his running abilities, but when it comes to scoring goals it's hard to find someone else more efficient than him.

Fantastic head

Even when the goal was empty, and the ball was at knee height, Klose chose to score his first goal with the national German team with his favorite weapon – his head – rather than just hit the ball with his foot towards the empty net.

Even he may not be remembered years from now, or receive the recognition he deserves, Klose will stand as one of the best attackers in headers and air plays.

He could score from any cross, high or low, and at any position regardless of who was playing against him. I remember the first day I heard of Klose, it was in 2002 during Germany's world cup game against KSA.

Before that day, Oliver Bierhoff was the king of air plays and the man whose head was made of gold, but all that changed when Klose scored the first, second, and fifth goals of the game that was the beginning of Klose's 16 world cup goals that made him the top scorer of the most appreciated championship in soccer.

Excellent positioning in crosses

Talking about headers, Klose scored 71 goals with the German national team, 54 of them – that's 76% - came from meeting crosses either with foot – 32 goals – or with headers – 22 goals. Most of these goals seemed easy – except for some of his fantastic headers, like the one against Netherlands – yet the key to all success is always simplicity.

Klose was a simple and extremely smart attacker, he didn't try to be someone he wasn't, he knew he was good at headers so he made himself a goal scoring machine that doesn't miss on a certain cross

The key to this was the way he positioned himself inside the penalty area, he was always one step ahead of the nearest defender, always before him when the ball comes at the near post, and behind him when the ball was played wide.

An excellent clue for how Klose was brilliant at positioning himself inside the area was the fact, every single one of the 16 goals Klose scored in the world cup was scored from 12 yards or less which.

He was great at reading the play and expecting where the ball will end so he can meet it with his foot or his head which gave him a special place in the hearts of all German people, despite not being praised for playing stylishly.

Andriy Shevchenko – The Siberian Tiger

Full Name: Andriy Mykolayovych Shevchenko

Date of birth: 29 September 1976

Nationality: Ukrainian

Status: Retired (2012), currently assistant manager for the Ukrainian National Team

Clubs: Dynamo Kyiv (Ukraine) – AC Milan (Italy) - Chelsea (England)

Goals scored and number of games: 369 goals in 759 games

Goals scored internationally: 48 goals in 111 Caps (All time goal scorer)

Club Trophies:

- UEFA Champions League: 2003 (AC Milan)
- UEFA Super Cup: 2003 (AC Milan)
- Italian League: 2003–04
- Ukrainian League: 5 Times
- Italian Cup (Coppa Italia): 2003
- English Cup (FA Cup): 2007
- Ukrainian Cup: 3 Times
- English League Cup: 2007
- Italian Super Cup (Supercoppa Italiana): 2004
- English Super Cup (Community Shield): 2009
- Ukrainian Super Cup: 2011

International trophies:

None

Personal trophies:

- Pele's List for the greatest 100 soccerers of all times.
- World Soccer's list of the 100 greatest soccerers in the 20th Century
- Ballon d'Or: 2004
- Italian foreign Soccerer of the year: 2000

- Italian League top scorer (Capocannoniere): Twice
- Ukrainian soccerer of the year: 6 Times
- Ukrainian League Golden Boot: 1998-99
- UEFA Champions League Top Scorer: Twice (7th top scorer of all times with 48 goals in 100 appearances)
- Ukraine all-time goal scorer
- Dynamo Kiev all-time goal scorer
- AC Milan second goal scorer of all times (175 goals in 322 appearances)

Career Overview

Andriy Shevchenko, or Sheva, started his career too early at the age of nine when he joined the youth system of one of Ukraine's biggest clubs of all times, Dynamo Kiev, with which he served for 5 consecutive years as an adult and helped the club establish itself as an emerging power in the European soccer during his first spell with the team between 1994 and 1999.

In 1990, 14 year-old Sheva won the Ian Rush Cup title, an invitation-based competition played between the youth academies of different European clubs. Sheva scored 9 that year and personally received the golden boot award from Liverpool's historical attacker.

Three years later, Sheva was gradually being pushed his coach, Yozhef Sabo, to take a major part with the team with which he made 17 appearances, all of them as a substitute, during his first year as a professional, with only one goal at his disposal.

However, the following year, 1996, was mystifying with Sheva scoring 16 goals in 31 league games and helping Dynamo win their second league title in a row as well as the domestic cup after defeating Nyva Vinnytsia 2-0.

He went on to score 72 goals during the next three seasons with the Ukrainian team and helped them add 3 more league titles, yet the highlight of his career with Dynamo was his European performance in 1998 when he helped the club defeat Barcelona 7-0 in the UEFA Champions league (3-0 and 4-0) including a hat-trick in the Camp Nou.

He then went on the following year, 1999, and became the tournament's top scorer after scoring 10 goals and helping Dynamo reach a European semi-final for the first time since 1987 but they eventually lost to Bayern Munich which later lost the final against Manchester United.

Milan

After being nominated for the 1999 Ballon d'Or award (he came third), Sheva was the target for many European giants, including Real Madrid.

Yet he chose to accept Silvio Berlusconi's $25 million offer and move to Italy to join AC Milan at the last summer before the second millennium.

In his first season with the club, Sheva proved himself as the real successor of Milan's icon, Marco Van Basten, and won the capocannonianeri trophy with 24 goals in 32 league-games and be the only player to do so since 1982.

Sheva then formed a magnificent duo with Juventus ex-star, Filippo Inzaghi, and they both helped Milan win the 2002-03 Champions League title after defeating Juventus in a penalty-shootout game in Old Trafford, before helping Milan win the league title in 2004 for the first time since 1998 and reach another European final.

The following year yet his dream for a second Champions league title evaporated as he missed a penalty in the famous 3-3 game against Liverpool that was later named as "The Miracle of Istanbul".

Looking for a new adventure after the disappointing loss against Liverpool, Sheva traveled, to London, to join the league's champions, Chelsea.

In 2006 after a huge pressure from both his wife and the club owner, Roman Abramovich, who saw in Sheva the key to transforming his club to a strong power not just in England, but also in Europe yet, things has shortly fallen apart.

Sheva spent an average first season with the Blues, scoring only 14 goals in 51 games, before suffering from a set of injuries that ruined the form he has just started to regain back early in 2007.

Such disappointment got him to move back on a loan deal to Milan however, the move wasn't successful so he broke it in 2009 and went back to Chelsea with which he played once before he decided it's time to move back to Ukraine and rejoin Dynamo Kiev before announcing his retirement 3 years later after winning the Ukrainian cup in 2011.

Performance Overview

His ability to sneak and approach the goal, while making the opponents what happened, is why he was named "The Siberian Tiger"

Supreme confidence

One of Sheva's best attributes is his ability to start the attack himself, and play solo at the front line, without the need of too much assisting. In fact some of his best goals started from the right wing, where he excelled best, with almost no teammate around him to help lessen the defensive pressure made on him.

Almost all attackers march towards the wing when they feel trapped and need more space, yet very a few of them who manage to get start the attack from the wing, dribble past few defenders and get the ball to the goal, especially when the one doing this thing is center forward, not a winger.

In Italy, it was only Sheva and Ronaldo who could do something with the ball even if surrounded by four, five or even six defenders.

The best demonstration for this was the wonderful goal he scored against Juventus in San Siro, he received the ball with four strong players around him, including the very quick, Edgar Davids.

Sheva went past them all towards his favorite right wing, before firing the ball from a dead angle towards Gianluigi Buffon's goal to score one of the best 10 goals to ever be scored in the Juve-Milan derby.

There is also his goal against Inter Milan, when the penalty area was crowded with 10 players yet he managed to dribble past the same defender twice before sending the ball towards the net despite being surrounded by six Inter defenders.

He rarely rushed a goal

Since Michel Platini joined Juventus in 1982, no one has ever won the Capocannoniere award – the Italian golden boot award – on his first season in the country except Andriy Shevchenko. This could be owed to the extreme poise and the solid sense of self-assurance he had in front of the goal.

In addition to his strong physique and his excellent use of his body that allowed him to compete and thrive in the world's most physically demanding league and against some of the strongest defenders in the world.

Sheva's ability to calmly make the best decision in front of the goal enabled him to be one of the best foreign attackers in Italy in the past 30, or even 50, years. If you ever watch Sheva's goals with Milan, you'll always notice this sense of timing I'm talking about.

Raul Gonzalez - El Niño

Full Name: Raul Gonzalez Blanco
Date of birth: 27 June 1977
Nationality: Spanish
Status: Retired (2015)
Clubs: Real Madrid (Spain) - Schalke (Germany) - Al Sadd (Qatar) - New York Cosmos (USA)
Goals scored and number of games: 430 goals in 1043 games
Goals scored internationally: 44 goals in 102 Caps

Club Trophies:
- UEFA Champions League: 3 Times (Real Madrid)
- UEFA Super Cup: 2002 (Real Madrid)
- Intercontinental Cup: Twice (Real Madrid)
- Spanish League: 6 Times
- Qatari League: 2012–13
- German Cup: 2011
- Qatari League Cup: 2014
- Spanish Super Cup: 4 Times
- German Super Cup: 2011

National team trophies:
None

Personal trophies:
- Pele's List for the greatest 100 soccerers of all times.
- Real Madrid record for making the most appearances with 741 games in 16 years
- Real Madrid number 2 goal scorer of all times with 323 goals (only Cristiano Ronaldo scored more goals for Madrid, with 360 goals in 344 appearances).

- Best Spanish player: 5 times (the only player to reach this number)
- Spanish League top goal scorer (Pichichi Trophy): Twice
- Champions League top scorer: 3 Times (and the third of all times with 71 goals in 142 games).
- Ballon d'Or: Second Place 2001

Career Overview

Born in San Cristóbal for a family that madly supports Atletico Madrid, Raul started playing soccer at the age of 10, in a local team, with only one goal in life, to play one day for Atletico Madrid and make his family proud.

Raul's dedication and strong work ethic made his dream almost come true and, at 3 years later, he was accepted in Atletico's youth system and was there for 2 years.

However, a strange decision from Atletico Madrid's president, Jesus Gil, to disband the entire system and release all young players for free got Raul to move in spring 1994 towards the enemy, Real Madrid, with which he kept progressing until he made his debut with the Spanish giant, 2 years later, against Real Zaragoza in the 29th of October 1994.

That day, Raul was asked by the Argentine legend and Real Madrid's manager, Jorge Valdano, if he was ready to make it to the first line-up to immediately answer him: If you want to win then play me, if you don't, then you can put someone else on the team.

With that type of mentality Raul, not only made his first debut that season, he continued to play alongside with Chile's attacker, Ivan Zamorano.

In 28 league games he scored 10 goals and won the Spanish Talent of the Year award. Raul became Valdano's first attacking option the following season to score 6 goals in Madrid's quest to win their first Champions League title since 1966.

Yet they failed to go past the quarter final after a 2-1 defeat to the, champion, Juventus.

Exploding in Madrid

Those 6 years between 1997 and 2003 were some of the most successful Madrid years since the 80s when the club won 5 league titles and 2 UEFA cups back to back. It first started when Madrid won the league title in 1996 with Raul being chosen as the league's best player.

Then Jorge Valdano resigned and Bayern's legendary coach, Jupp Heynckes, became the new manager in 1997, and with new players in the team like Davor Suker, and Raul's U-20 teammate, Fernando Morientes, Madrid won their first Champions League title (7th European Cup) in 1998 thanks to Predrag Mijatovic's 66th minute goal against Juventus in Amsterdam Arena.

The following year Raul won the Pichichi award with his 25 league goals before helping Madrid win the last Champions League title of the millennia after defeating the neighbor, Valencia, 3-0 in a game that witnessed Raul scoring his famous 75th minute run against Valencia's defense.

Raul was the tournament's top scorer the following year 2000-01, before scoring in the final to help Madrid defeat Bayer Leverkusen in the 2001-02 final.

During these six years, Raul was chosen as the best player in the country 5 times (including 4 in a row) as he scored 157 goals in all competitions, and helped Madrid win 9 titles including 3 league titles and one European super cup in 2002.

The Galacticos Period

Florentino Perez's plans to make the club the best in the world were catastrophic.

Despite winning the league title twice in 2007 and 2008, the club's performance both domestically and internationally declined dramatically.

This mainly because the president of the club, Perez, decided to buy players that can sell shirts, like Michael Owen, over players who can win trophies like Claude Makélélé, the best defensive midfielder of his generation who was sold to Chelsea in 2003 because he couldn't score goals!

The atmosphere wasn't positive in the dressing room, with the old guards feeling second-tiered, and Raul's performance was affected by the mess the club was getting itself into.

He scored 52 goals during the following 4 seasons with Madrid failing to qualify beyond the round of 16 in the famous European championship.

However, he regained his form after the departure of Fabio Capello, and scored 23 goals to help Madrid win the 2007-08 league title, 18 points above Barcelona.

Raul then spent two more years with the club yet all the attacking roles went to young players like Gonzalo Higuaín, and the 2 newcomers Cristiano Ronaldo, and Karim Benzema.

He decided to leave to Shalke 04 with which he spent 2 magnificent seasons scoring 40 goals, and helping the German club win 2 domestic titles before he left to Qatar for 2 years, and retired in USA in 2015.

Performance Overview

Not the fastest, not the hardest shooting one, not the strongest one, but probably the wisest one…

A different mindset

If you want to win then play me, if you don't, then you can put someone else on the team.

This is what 17 year-old Raul said to his first Real Madrid coach, Jorge Valdano, the night before he made his debut with Madrid's first team.

As discussed later by Valdano, the Argentine coach wanted to make sure his young player wasn't nervous before playing his first game with the team, yet what he heard made him sure he was in front of an extraordinary young player who later went on to break Alfredo Di Stefano's record as the club's all-time goal scorer.

Physically, Raul wasn't the strongest, and technically, Raul wasn't the most gifted but as described by one of his early coaches, he was the one with the highest work rate, he trained before games, after games, and on weekends, and since a very young age, he was always the first one on the training field.

With such tenacity and self-discipline, it was easier for Raul to maintain his confidence and poise at some of the difficult times in his career with Real Madrid and maintain his mark with a club known for not being mercy with non-performing players.

Clever and Focused

He –Raul - always had the edge above his opponents in the area. His thinking was quicker than them. Jorge Valdano, on his young player

Like I said earlier, Raul wasn't the most talented, yet by far, he was the cleverest attacker in Spain during the time he played for Madrid.

He was focused and had the gift of reading defenders and goalkeepers, and predicting both their moves and mistakes accurately.

In many cases, he seemed to know what defenders will do and how keepers would react, this resulted in many chip goals including his famous Santiago Bernabéu goal against Valencia and the other 18 yard chip he scored against Malaga in the Spanish League.

I always think about goals, it's the only most important thing in the match. It was always on my mind to look for a chance, a half chance or a defensive error.

Hristo Stoichkov - The Pitbull

Full Name: Hristo Stoichkov Stoichkov

Date of birth: 8 February 1966

Nationality: Bulgarian

Status: Retired (2003)

Clubs: Hebros Harmanli, CSKA Sofia (Bulgaria) - Chicago Fire, D.C. United (USA) - Barcelona (Spain) - Parma (Italy) - Al-Nassr (KSA) - Kashiwa Reysol (Japan)

Goals scored and number of games: 723 goals in 771 games

Goals scored internationally: 37 goals in 83 Caps

Club Trophies:

- UEFA Champions League (European Cup): 1991-92 (Barcelona)
- UEFA Cup Winners' Cup: 1996–97 (Barcelona)
- European Super Cup: Twice (Barcelona)
- Spanish League: 5 Times
- Bulgarian League: 3 Times (CSKA Sofia)
- Spanish Cup (Copa del Rey): 1996–97
- Bulgarian Cup: 4 Times (CSKA Sofia)
- Spanish Super Cup: 3 Times
- Bulgarian Super Cup: 1989 (CSKA Sofia
- Asian Cup Winners Cup: 1998 (Al-Nassr)

National team trophies:

- FIFA World Cup: Semi Final 1994

Personal trophies:

- Pele's List for the greatest 100 soccerers of all times.
- World Soccer's 100 Greatest Players of the 20th Century
- FIFA World Cup Golden Shoe: 1994

- Ballon d'Or: 1994
- Onze d'Or: 1992
- Bulgarian Soccerer of the Year: 5 Times
- European Golden Shoe: 1990
- Best foreign player in Spain (Don Balón Award): 1994

Career Overview

Born at a small village that was later named after him, Stoichkov started his career in a small team in Bulgaria, called FC Herbos, a team he joined at the age of 16 and left two years later to join the country's biggest club, CSKA Sofia.

Stoichkov journey was CSKA was starting well, as the young player scored 11 appearances in his first year including the Bulgarian cup final against Levski Sofia.

However, a late fight with Levski's midfielder, Emil Spasov, resulted in a red card and life-time ban for the young attacker whose career had to end before it even began. Three months later, however, the ban was reduced and Stoichkov was set to get back to play after nine months.

Mystifying with CSKA

It seemed like the lesson was learned, and the 20 year old kid has now grown up scoring 7 during his first year before exploding with 104 during the following 3 season.

During this period, Stoichkov helped CSKA win 2 league titles, 3 cups back to back, as well reach the 1989 European Cups Winners' cup semi-finals.

However, they lost to Barcelona 6-3 and Stoichkov was signed to replace Gary Lineker after his marvelous performance and the 3 goals he scored against the Catalan team, including a famous chip-over goal in Camp Nou.

Barca's first dream team

Now that they haven't won the league since 1984, Barcelona's new manager, Johan Cruyff, took it on his shoulders to completely transform the Catalan team and bring it back to competing once again.

He started this by signing Michael Laudrop from Juventus, before signing Stoichkov ,and ascending Guardiola from the second team, the following year to succeed at building what is now known as Barcelona's first dream team.

That team, whose cherry was Stoichkov, went on to win 4 consecutive league titles, 2 Spanish cups, and 3 European finals including the 1992 European cup and the super cup for the same year.

Stoichkov scored 106 goals during that period including the opener in Super Cup game against Werder Bremen in the year 1992, the same year he won the Onze d'Or, as the best player in Europe.

World Cup

Nobody, not even a single citizen, expected Bulgaria to qualify to the 1994 world cup on behalf of France with its stars Cantona, Papin and Laurent Blanc.

France entered the last game of the group stage, with 2 points ahead of Bulgaria and was even relieved when Eric Cantona scored an early opener in the first half.

Yet, a double from Emil Kostadinov, including a 90 minute winner, got Bulgaria to qualify in Paris and in front of 48,000 supporters in PSG's stadium, Parc des Princes.

Stoichkov, and his team, then flew to Chicago to play their group stage games against Argentina, Greece and Nigeria.

Despite a strange 3-0 loss against Nigeria, the Bulgarians pulled themselves together and scored 6 goals in 2 games, half of them for Stoichkov, including a 2-0 win against Argentina.

They then met Mexico in the second round, and the game went to a penalty shootout despite Stoichkov's early opener, yet, to his own luck, he didn't bother himself scoring his final penalty kick as Bulgaria ended the shootout at a score of 3-1.

And now after qualifying to the quarter final, Bulgaria had to face the former champion, Germany in a game that witnessed Stoichkov scoring a late equalizing from a fantastic free kick before his teammate, Yordan Letchkov, score a header only 12 minutes before the end of the game to qualify Bulgaria for the first, and only time, to the semifinal of a major tournament.

However the journey ended with Roberto Baggio scoring a double for Italy to eliminate the Bulgarians from the semifinal, despite Stoichkov first-half penalty.

Parma and Barcelona

Looking for a new challenge after winning the 1994 Ballon d'Or, Stoichkov moved to Parma in 1995, to help prepare what would later be known as Parma's historical team.

Despite spending only one team with the Italian club before moving back to Catalonia, Stoichkov's personality and leadership skills affected players like Guianluigi Buffon and Fabio Cannavaro, and helped Parma make its best performance ever in the Italian league after finishing second, only 2 points behind Juventus.

After that, Stoichkov spent two years, in his second spell with Barcelona, in which he won the league title with Luis Van Gaal as well as the 1997 UEFA Cup Winners' cup against PSG before he left to Bulgaria for a short, second, spell with CSKA Sofia.

Performance Overview

When he woke up on the right side of the pillow and had a good day, no defender in the world could stop him from scoring.

A born-leader

The confidence in his own skills, and the winning mentality he possessed, all convinced a man like Johan Cruyff to make him the captain of Barcelona, and the brain around which all playing was constructed. Stoichkov was a naturally-born leader, with the ability to lead and keep his sanity under the toughest of circumstances.

In fact, when being questioned whether he signed amazing Stoichkov for the goal the Bulgarian scored against Barcelona in the Champions League, Johan Cruyff said the following words:

I chose to sign Hristo, not because of his goals but, for his character and mentality. He has a hard, but strong, character, and I badly needed a player with such a personality in my team.

The best example for Stoichkov's leadership, though, is was what he did with Bulgaria in the 1994 World Cup.

On their first game in the tournament, Bulgaria received a major hit when they lost 3-0 against the supposedly weak team of Nigeria.

But what happened next was almost a miracle as he took the team to a crucial win against Greece before scoring against Argentina in their last and must-win group stage game to help them qualify for the first time to the round of 16.

Well there, he scored against Mexico and then Germany in the quarter final game to make history with the Bulgarian team who reached the semifinal of the tournament for the first and last time in their history.

One of the acts showing how a winner Stoichkov was, is when he paid for a man working at the Mexican camp to bring a list of all players participating in their round of 16 game, including all the information regards the game tactics and the penalty-shooting order.

Bulgaria then went on to defeat Mexico on a penalty shootout with the first three penalties missed by the Mexican team.

Fast with excellent shot accuracy

To shortly summarize Stoichkov's career with Barcelona, we could say he was one of the best "thieves" in the soccer world. His quick, short legs, and his ability to hold onto the ball without losing it made him a key player in Johan Cruyff's dream team in the early 90s.

During his Barcelona days, Stoichkov excelled best when he was given the freedom to use his speed and switch between the wings and the AM role, actually, just a look at his goal against Athletic Bilbao in Barcelona's 6-0 win at San Mamés.

He scored participated in all six goals with his shots and assists, but the best of them all was the run he made in the third goal when he received the ball near the center and ran from the wing to deep in the middle before scoring in front of 4 defenders.

Excellent left foot

Stoichkov was also one of the best lefties I've ever seen, he was able to score from anywhere, and any position using his left, golden foot that was so accurate at shooting that he was one of the feared free-kick takers in Europe during the time he spent in Spain, and the player responsible for all types of set pieces in the Catalan team.

His remarkable touch against Argentina, the strike against Mexico in the round of 16, and the amazing free kick against Germany in the quarterfinals of the 1994 World cup all were played by his left foot.

David Villa - El Guaje (The Kid)

Full Name: David Villa Sanchez

Date of birth: 3 December 1981

Nationality: Spanish

Status: Currently playing (Melbourne City FC), Sporting Gijón, Real Zaragoza, Valencia, Barcelona, Atlético Madrid (Spain) - New York City (USA) - Melbourne City (Australia)

Goals scored and number of games: 365 goals in 737 games (and counting)

Goals scored internationally: 59 goals in 97 Caps (All-time top scorer)

Club trophies:

- UEFA Champions League: 2010-11 (Barcelona)
- UEFA Super Cup: 2011 (Barcelona)
- FIFA Club World Cup: 2011(Barcelona)
- Spanish League (La Liga): 3 Times (Barcelona & Atlético Madrid)
- Spanish Cup (Copa del Rey): 3 Times (Barcelona, Real Zaragoza & Valencia)
- Spanish Super Cup (Supercopa de España): 3 Times (Real Zaragoza & Barcelona)

National team trophies:

- FIFA World Cup: Gold Medal (2010)
- UEFA European Championship: EURO 2008

Personal trophies:

- EURO 2008 Golden Boot
- Best Spanish player of the year: 2005-06
- 2010 FIFA World Cup Silver Shoe
- Onze d'Or (Best player in Europe): Twice 1986, 1987
- FIFA U-20 World Cup: Best player 1979

Career Overview

Villa started his professional career playing for Sporting Gijón with which he scored 41 goals in the 2 seasons he spent in the Spanish second division but despite such record, Villa had to leave the club after finishing 10th on the league table and failing to promote to La Liga.

In summer 2003, Villa joined Real Zaragoza in a 3 million-Euros deal to help the Spanish underdog win the 2004 Copa del Rey title on his first season with the team followed by a 3-2 win in the Spanish Super Cup against Valencia, the club he will later join for $16 million in summer 2005.

Valencia

Villa exploded and mystified in Valencia, forming a strong companionship with Spain and Real Madrid ex-player, Fernando Morientes, to score 40 goals in their first season together before helping Valencia win the Spanish Cup after defeating Getafe 3-1.

Such performance got Luis Aragones choose his make a controversial and strange decision and pick Villa over Real Madrid and Spain's all-time goal scorer, Raul Gonzalez, to be his key attacker in the Spanish squad heading to compete for the 2008 European Championship.

That summer, Villa proved his maven coach to be right as he scored a hat-trick on his first game against Russia before finishing the tournament as a European champion, as well as the tournament's top goal scorer with 4 goals. Villa then spent two amazing seasons with Valencia, scoring 59 goals in all tournaments and placing himself as the best successor for both Thierry Henry and Zlatan Ibrahimović who were both heading out of the club in 2010.

Barcelona

Despite not maintaining the same goal scoring rate with Barcelona, Villa proved himself as a versatile player when he joined Barcelona in summer 2010, right after winning his second golden boot award. But this time in the African world cup which he helped Spain win after scoring 5 goals, including a late quarter-final winner against Paraguay.

With Barcelona, Villa was the key forward in Pep Guardiola's squad to help, alongside Pedro and Bojan Krkić, in providing assistance to the team's star Lionel Messi, and in his 3 years with the Catalan club, Villa helped the team win every trophy possible, including the Champions League and the Club World Cup titles of the year 2011.

Villa then moved to join Diego Simeone's squad in 2013 and helped Atletico Madrid win the Spanish league as well as qualify for the second time in their history to the Champions League final game which they lost to Real Madrid in 2014.

Performance

In my opinion, David Villa, is one of the most underrated goal scorers and one of the greatest attackers I have ever seen, and here are my reasons:

He can play anywhere and still shine

Anywhere he had gone, Villa shined. From Sporting Gijón to New York City FC, Villa proved himself in every single team he played regardless of the overall performance of the team. Except for his period in Barcelona, Villa's confidence and goal scoring skills enabled him to become the man behind the whole show in all the teams he played for. For instance what he did with Real Zaragoza in 2003 was admirable.

They bought him from Gijón the following year after they have been promoted to the first division (La Liga) and in two years with the team he was responsible for scoring 52 goals, including his fantastic finish against Racing Santander, before scoring against Real Madrid and helping the club win the Spanish cup, and their only second domestic cup in 10 years.

Even when went to Atletico Madrid, when everybody thought it was time for him to quit soccer or play outside Europe he proved himself worthy and was one of reasons why Madrid won its first league title since 1995 after scoring 15 goals in 2013, including a fantastic, first-timer against Barcelona in Vicente Calderón.

Even today, when everyone is blaming Frank Lampard for moving to America and making a joke of himself, Villa is still on fire with New York City FC, and being picked as the club's player of the season with 18 goals in his 30 appearances with the team.

He can adapt at any attacking position

Probably the one Zlatan Ibrahimović regrets the most is leaving Barcelona the same year they won the Champions league title because he couldn't accept shadowing Messi and changing his style to be more of a team player.

I agree that Ibrahimović is a unique player with a unique style, yet I must also respect the talented, Villa, who managed to fit in Barcelona's arsenal and, successfully, took the role Ibra has previously denied.

Back with Valencia, Villa was the leader of the orchestra and the team star who had the freedom to play anywhere he wanted upfront, and lead a team of stars like David Silva and Juan Mata to win the, 2007-08, Spanish Cup.

He could play as a playmaker, a striker or a shadow striker to Fernando Morientes, and managed to keep a rate of 26 goals per season. Yet, unlike Ibra, he found no problem taking different, less elusive, duties in Barcelona with Messi taking all credit.

In 3 years with Barcelona, Villa contributed more to the team than to himself, scoring 48 goals in 120 games and winning every single trophy a soccer player would dream of, including the European title in 2011 when he scored the third in a 3-0 win against Manchester United.

Overwhelmingly Complete

David Villa had it all, he's fast, he can dribble, he's a penalty-kick specialist, can shoot from anywhere on the field and has a head of gold that can score from anywhere inside the penalty area.

Try to watch his best goals with all the teams he played for, and not only you'll see his performance curve going up over the years, you'll also see excellent, and fancy goals, scored from all positions and with all styles.

For me, his goal against Real Madrid in the Bernabéu is his best ever. Simply the way he twisted his body to kick the ball and make it chip a little bit above Iker Casillas's hands was exceptional. I highly encourage you to watch this goal.

Mario Kempes - Matador

Full Name: Mario Alberto Kempes
Date of birth: 15 July 1954
Nationality: Argentine
Status: Retired 1999
Clubs: Instituto, Rosario Central, River Plate (Argentina) - Valencia, Hércules (Spain) - First Vienna, St. Pölten, Kremser SC (Austria) - Fernández Vial (Chile) - Pelita Jaya (Indonesia)
Goals scored and number of games: 320 goals in 592 games
Goals scored internationally: 20 goals in 43 Caps
Club Trophies:
- UEFA Cup Winners' Cup: 1980 (Valencia)
- UEFA Super Cup: 1980
- Argentine Premier Division: 1981 (River Plate)
- Spanish Cup (Copa del Rey): 1978- 79 (Valencia)

National team trophies:
- FIFA World Cup: Gold Medal (1978)

Personal trophies:
- Pele's List for the greatest 100 soccerers of all times.
- FIFA World Cup Golden Ball: 1978
- FIFA World Cup Golden Boot: 1978
- Spanish League top scorer (Pichichi award): Twice
- Onze d'Or (Best player in Europe): 1978
- South American soccerer of the year: 1978

Career Overview

Encouraged by his father, Kempes started playing soccer at the age of 7 before joining the youth team of the local club, Instituto Atlético.

With them, he scored 11 goals in the club's first ever appearance in the Argentine's first division to grab the attention of Rosario Central which signed the young talent in summer 1974.

In Rosario, it took 20 year-old Kempes one season to become Argentine's top scorer and help the club win the Metropolitan before dramatically losing the title after finishing only one point behind San Lorenzo, the champion.

Such performance enabled him a place in the Argentine squad heading to West Germany for the 1974 yet, the unexpected happened, and Kempes failed to score any goal and Argentina left the tournament early after being trashed by both Netherlands and Brazil at the second round.

Kempes, now nicknamed as El Matador, kept his fantastic, domestic, performance with Rosario, scoring 56 goals in only one and a half season before making a move to Spain, to join the 1971 league champion, in January, 1976.

Valencia

Kempes didn't impress much at his beginning with Valencia as he failed to score any in his first 5 games with the team.

Yet he sooner kept all doubts at bay and finished his first season with the bats as the league's Pichichi with 24 goals in 34 league games before doing it again the following season and finishing his preparation for the Argentine world cup as the top goal scorer for both the La Liga, and the Spanish Cup which he helped Valencia win after defeating Real Madrid 2-0.

Kempes then flew to Argentina to help Argentina win their first ever world cup title after defeating Netherlands 3-1 in the final game.

In that tournament, and despite not scoring any goal in the group stage, Kempes scored a double against both Poland and Peru, to help Argentina finish on top of its 2nd round group stage with only 3 goals above Brazil – both teams had 5 points – and qualify to the final game against Netherlands.

And in June 25th, 1978 and in front of 71,000 raving Argentine fans in the Monumental Stadium, Kempes scored twice and assisted once to help Argentina become the third South American team, after Uruguay and Brazil, to ever win the world cup.

After winning the Onze d'Or, thanks to his performance in the world cup, Kempes went back to Valencia where he helped the club win its first ever European championship after defeating Arsenal, on penalties, in the 1980 UEFA Cup Winners' cup, before defeating Nottingham Forrest in the European Super cup 3 months later.

Argentina – Spain back and forth

Kempes moved back to Argentina for only one year where he helped River Plate win the premier division before he decided to move back to Valencia where he spent two more years scoring 24 goals and making himself the club's 3rd goal scorer of all times.

Performance

Kempes was great at scoring with his feet as well as with his head.

The Storming Matador

Alongside with Gabriel Batistuta, Mario Kempes remains one of Argentine few attackers who combine between their strong physique and their excellent technical skills. Nicknamed with El Matador, Kempes was known for his daring nature and his ability to storm, sometimes carelessly, between defenders.

He wasn't afraid to get hit or lose the ball, and knew it's probably the best way to surprise the opponents was by taking the shortest route to the goal and storming at it right from the center of the penalty area. His 2 goals, for instance, against Netherlands in the world cup final demonstrated this theme clearly.

In the first one, and rather than complete a 1-2 pass with Leopoldo Luque, he went ahead towards the goal, not caring with the defender next to him. The even upped to this in the second goal when he stormed alone inside the Dutch area and kept fighting solo until he scored Argentina's winner.

Winning comes first

Like Diego Simeone who would throw a second ball into the field to stop attacks against Atletico Madrid, to Maradona who used "the hand of God" to score against England in the 1986 world cup.

It seems the Argentine love winning so dearly that they wouldn't mind breaking some laws to win a game, and Mario Kempes wasn't an exception. His daring personality and his love for winning had emerged themselves on his playing style.

He would use force against any defender who dares to hit one of his teammates, he would fake penalties and was known for sending spies to bring him the latest news regards the opposite teams' tactics and formations during the time as a manager and even before that, when he used to play for Valencia.

One of his memorable incidents though was the one that got Argentina to avoid being eliminated from the round of 8 in the 1978 world cup when the Argentine team had no option but to defeat Poland and Kempes used his fist to box the ball away from the goal line and turned it to a penalty kick that was saved by Argentina's goalkeeper, Ubaldo Fillol.

Gary Lineker – Sir

Full Name: Gary Winston Lineker
Date of birth: 30 November 1960
Nationality: English
Status: Retired 1994
Clubs: Leicester City, Everton, Tottenham Hotspur (England) - Barcelona (Spain) - Nagoya Grampus Eight (Japan)
Goals scored and number of games: 329 goals in 647 games
Goals scored internationally: 48 goals in 80 Caps
Club Trophies:

-   European Cup Winners' Cup: 1989 (Barcelona)
-   Spanish Cup (Copa del Rey) :1988
-   English Cup (FA Cup): 1990-91 (Tottenham Hotspur)
-   English Super Cup (Charity Shield): 1984-85 (Everton)

Personal trophies:

-   Pele's List for the greatest 100 soccerers of all times.
-   English soccerer of the year: Twice
-   Ballon d'Or: Second Place 1986
-   English League top scorer: 3 Times
-   FIFA World Cup Golden Boot: 1986

Career Overview

The highly disciplined who received no cards, not even a yellow one, throughout the 18 years he played....

In 1986, Lineker joined the league champion, Everton to win his second golden boot title, yet his 30 league goals were not enough to help the Toffees win their 9th league title which went to their city neighbors and rivals, Liverpool with only 2 points in difference.

Such performance, added to the 6 goals he scored in the Mexican world cup, grabbed the attention of the Spanish giants, Barcelona, who made him an offer he couldn't refuse to leave Everton after spending only one year with the club, and join Barcelona in a four year deal.

In Barcelona

Linkere wasn't lucky to join Barcelona at a thriving time like the one we're currently witnessing. He only caught the early beginning of Johan Cruyff's managerial period with the team and was dismissed for not being versatile enough to play on the wing rather than in the center of the attacking line.

However, and during his first 2 seasons with Barcelona, Lineker was the team's star, scoring 41 goals for Luis Aragonés's side, including a hat-trick against Real Madrid and the capturing of the Spanish cup inside the Santiago Bernabéu stadium after defeating Real Sociedad 1-0 in spring 1988.

Lineker then moved to London to join Tottenham Hotspur with which he won a third golden boot thanks to the 24 goals he scored for the Spurs that helped them finish third on the league table for the first time in more than 25 years.

The following year though, Lineker won himself a penalty in Spurs win against Nottengham Forrest in the FA cup final to help the North Londoners win their 8th and last FA Cup title in their history before coming only one goal behind Arsenal's Ian Wright in the 1991-92 goal-scoring table.

That season was the last for Lineker in England as he flew to Tokyo, Japan in which he played for Nagoya Grampus FC before announcing his early retirement in 1994.

Performance Overview

A gentleman on the soccer field while at the same time deadly posing when he found himself either outside or outside the 18 yard box.

Agile

Speeding a defender towards the ball has always been Lineker forte. He was able to outrun any defender no matter who he was using his quick short legs that allowed him to score many goals, including the second goal he scored against Poland in the Mexican world cup.

That day, Lineker was under pressure to score for England as it has been 6 games since the last time he scored for the team. He scored the first goal from a short cross, yet what he did in the second goal was remarkable.

The ball was thrown on the left wing to Nottingham Forest's Steve Hodge who was the only player with Lineker in the Polish half, and before Hodge has even reached the ball, or get himself close to the box, Gary Lineker has already sprinted and took his position past 2 defenders to direct his teammate's excellent cross into the net.

Classic

Lineker was a classic, fox-in-the-box, type of attackers. His greatest assets were his finishing style, headers, and the way he positioned himself inside the penalty area that was so smart to the extent that it made most of his goals look ordinary.

It's important to understand that the fact he couldn't excel at Cruyff's tiki-taka style shouldn't disqualify Lineker as a prolific attacker. Zlatan Ibrahimović, himself, failed to adapt to Pep Guardiola's style at Barcelona yet he's still one of the greatest players to ever play soccer.

Like Ibra, Lineker too was a top notch player who found his mastery inside the box as he fed on lost balls and follow ups.

In fact, the 3 goals he scored against Real Madrid in Barcelona's 3-2 win in 1987 were, exactly, what anyone can expect from a classic center forward.

The first was a short cross where he has beaten the defender to the ball and touched it from inside the 6-yard area. The second was quite similar, and also from inside the 6 yards, as he followed up a ball deflected from Madrid's goalkeeper and sent it towards the empty net.

The third however was somehow different, but with no magic, as he received a lost ball from one of Madrid's defenders, moved with the ball a few meters before sending it above the goalkeeper.

A typical, smart, classical, attacker, who knew pretty well how to do his job.

Ending...

So, the question remains: Is it realistic for you to expect to become a great soccer player?

I'll be straight with you....

I don't know

That would be like trying to judge a picture without even looking at it. I don't know what attributes do you have, how prepared are you mentally, or how strong do you believe in yourself and your ability to improve.

But here's a thing

If you neglect anything you don't have right now, and commit yourself to mastering what you do have control over, you can absolutely become a great player.

Of course, you might not be sure of having what it takes to become a professional soccer player. You may think it's too late to start or there are too many things you lack.

This may be true, but let me tell you a story about a man, a 29 year old guy, who was told he didn't have what it takes to make it as a player. He was jailed twice, and spent some of his best career days taking 12-hour shifts in a brick factory.

This man who started playing professional soccer at the age of 23 is called Jamie Vardy, and he's now the leading goal scorer of the English premier league, and one step away from winning the league with Leicester City, the team that escaped relegation only two weeks before the end of the last season, anyway.

Soccer is just like any other skill, it requires hours and hours of working on your craft until you master your own game.

The problem?

People don't like to work hard.

At least the majority of them

So what to do?

Make your desire burn so big that the buzz of working hard is about as noticeable as an ant to an elephant. Dream so big, and apply yourself with gusto and excitement and take actions everyday towards your new vision and you'll make it. Just focus on the things you can do today and work on doing it, day after the other, and you'll see a big difference.